RAILWAYS IN NORTHUMBERL

Alan Young

Class K1 No 62011 about to leave Alnwick for Alnmouth in June 1966, the final month of steam operation on the branch. *(Verdun Wake / J W Armstrong Trust Collection)*

Published by Martin Bairstow, 53 Kirklees Drive, Farsley, Leeds
Printed by The Amadeus Press, Cleckheaton, West Yorkshire

Introduction

Northumberland, England's most northerly county, has dramatically contrasting landscapes. The southeast corner, corresponding to one of Britain's largest coalfields, and dominated by Newcastle upon Tyne, is densely populated. The valleys of the rivers North and South Tyne, combining their waters near Hexham, are largely idyllic, pastoral countryside, with a scattering of attractive villages and small towns. North of the coalfield is an expanse of sparsely populated, undulating farmland, stretching to the River Tweed. From the South Tyne to the Tweed, the western border with Cumbria and Scotland has some of England's wildest country. It consists of vast tracts of moorland, rising to the Cheviot (2676ft), a remote expanse of peat bog. The coast has a series of bays with sandy beaches and dunes, enhanced by Dunstanburgh and Bamburgh castles; the Farne Islands and Holy Island are offshore. Almost two thousand years ago, Hadrian's Wall was constructed from Wallsend-on-Tyne to the Solway, and impressive sections still remain. The empty landscape in the upper North Tyne valley was twice transformed in the Twentieth Century; from the 1930s Kielder Forest was planted, a huge swathe of conifers, and in the 1970s Kielder Water reservoir was created. These landscape management projects have given us the largest forest and artificial lake in Britain.

The county has a long history of railway development. From the early 17th Century, numerous waggonways were constructed in the coalfield, and a network of passenger lines developed during the 19th Century, focussed on Newcastle. The Newcastle-Carlisle line was the first east-to-west coast railway in Britain; it possesses a splendid collection of architectural relics from the pioneering railway era. The East Coast main line, host to streamlined Pacifics, then Deltics, Inter-City 125s, and now Class 91 electrics, has a stretch of over sixty miles in Northumberland. Delightful branch lines, most of them hopelessly uneconomic, linked isolated communities to the main lines. Some of the loneliest countryside was served by the North British Railway, a Scottish company intent on reaching Newcastle.

Passenger railway closures began early in Northumberland. Some sixty miles, almost a fifth of the network, closed before 1931. Most of the minor rural lines had closed when, in 1962 aged eleven, I resolved to visit the remaining routes. I am grateful to my parents for allowing me to make unaccompanied journeys from home in Longbenton to such destinations as Newbiggin, Alnwick, North Wylam, and Alston. Runabout and Day Line Diesel tickets made these trips affordable. A few weeks' pocket money was spent on a 'special' to Woodburn. My particular regret is failing to reach Kelso by train, thanks to oversleeping on the day of my planned visit! Since the early 1970s I have visited most lines and stations (open and closed) in the British Isles to photograph what is left, and found that Northumberland is especially rich in railway architecture and relics.

Railways of Northumberland is a companion to *Suburban Railways of Tyneside*, therefore the 'Metro' area is referred to only in passing in the present volume. Northumberland's boundaries are treated liberally, to include Alston and Carlisle (Cumberland), Riccarton Junction and Kelso (Roxburghshire), and the Durham bank of the Tyne west of Gateshead. The focus is particularly on the railway routes and stations, rather than motive power, rolling stock, signalling and accidents, which other writers have covered comprehensively.

In preparing this book I have used resources in the Public Record Office (Kew), Northumberland Record Office (Gosforth), the Ken Hoole Study Centre (Darlington), and York City Archive. I wish to thank the staff for their help. I am also grateful to Martin Bairstow, Ken Groundwater, Alan Thompson, John Petrie, Alan Wells, and John Addyman for information and encouragement. Particular thanks are due to my wife, Sue, for her patience as I have devoted much time to this project. Information has been drawn from various published sources; these are listed in the bibliography.

Alan Young
Southfield, Lancashire. February 2003

The author (in anorak!) at Featherstone Park station on the Alston Branch, in May 1966. *(Martin Young)*

The East Coast Main Line

On 5 July 1952 Class A4 4-6-2 No 60024 *Kingfisher* enters Newcastle Central with the *Flying Scotsman* service from London King's Cross. It is scheduled to leave at 3.11 pm for Edinburgh Waverley.
(J W Armstrong Trust)

Eastern Northumberland provided an easy north-south route, interrupted only by the deep, narrow valleys of the rivers Blyth, Wansbeck, Coquet and Aln, and the wider Tweed valley. The Great North Road followed this corridor, and from the 1830s there were schemes to build a parallel railway between Newcastle and Berwick. The Grand Eastern (1837) and Great North British (1839) railways were unsuccessful, partly because of opposition from Morpeth tradesmen whose town the lines bypassed.

In 1844 Tyneside and London were directly linked by rail. Two years later the North British Railway pushed south from Scotland to Berwick. Two rival proposals to close the gap between Newcastle and Berwick came before Parliament in 1844. Isambard Kingdom Brunel ('Father of the Great Western Railway') proposed that the **Northumberland Railway** should pass through South Gosforth, Blagdon, Morpeth, Widdrington, Lesbury, Embleton, and Chathill. He planned to use his atmospheric traction system, already installed on the Dublin & Kingstown and London-Croydon railways, to propel trains. The **Newcastle & Berwick Railway**, backed by George Hudson ('The Railway King') with technical support from George Stephenson, was the other proposal; this scheme obtained the Royal Assent on 21 July 1845. In the early 1840s the North British Railway was preparing to open its Edinburgh-

Berwick route, and, in 1847, Hudson attempted to add this company to his portfolio. The history of Northumbrian railways would have been very different had he succeeded!

The N&B opened from Heaton to Morpeth on 1 March 1847. Chathill-Tweedmouth opened on 29 March, followed by Morpeth-Chathill on 1 July 1847. Hudson had shrewdly merged the N&B with the Newcastle & North Shields Railway in 1844, allowing the main line to share the N&NS Carliol Square terminus in Newcastle and two miles of the North Shields branch to Heaton. This explains why the ECML leaves Newcastle as if bound for Tynemouth, before a broad curve through a rural area takes it northwards into Newcastle's outer suburbs at Forest Hall. The line follows an indirect route north to Morpeth. Neighbouring collieries with enormous pit-heaps were linked to the ECML by mineral lines and sidings. By the late-1970s most collieries and sidings had disappeared, and Killingworth and Cramlington new towns were added to the landscape of Victorian mining villages. Between Plessey and Stannington a viaduct crosses the Blyth valley. Entering Morpeth the ECML has a tight curve. This site has witnessed four accidents, three caused by drivers ignoring speed restrictions.

After Morpeth the River Wansbeck is crossed, then, for several miles, the route is again indirect as

3

it follows the most level course and misses most of the area's villages. Alnwick, central Northumberland's principal market town, is three miles west of the ECML. The grounds of Alnwick Castle lay across any potential route through the town, and the Duke of Northumberland would not permit a railway to violate them. Alnwick was served by Lesbury station, but in 1850 a branch from Bilton Junction (Alnmouth from 1892) reached Alnwick, its terminus a safe distance south of the castle. At Alnmouth the northbound ECML passenger at last glimpses the sea, beyond the sandy estuary of the River Aln. North of Alnmouth a viaduct crosses the Aln. The journey continues through pleasant, thinly populated countryside. On this gently graded route, the steepest stretch (2¼ miles at 1 in 150) is encountered at Christon Bank, falling northwards. Near Beal there is a distant view of Holy Island with its castle and derelict priory. Sand dunes flank the route at Goswick, followed by sea cliffs at Scremerston. Approaching Berwick the passenger is treated to one of the highlights of British railway travel: the **Royal Border Bridge.** The bridge seems misnamed. Since 1482 the Anglo-Scottish border has been at Marshall Meadows, two miles north of Berwick. However the names 'Tweed Bridge' and 'Berwick Bridge' had already been used for a 17th Century road crossing. In August 1847 the N&B amalgamated with the York & Newcastle Railway, and the newly-created York, Newcastle & Berwick Railway was responsible for bridging the Tweedmouth-Berwick gap. The foundation stone was laid on 15 May 1847 (under N&B administration). The bridge opened to freight on 20 July 1850. The formal opening to passenger trains was performed by Queen Victoria on 29 August 1850. The 720yd stone and brick structure is slightly curved, carries two tracks, and possesses 28 arches, each of 61ft 6in span. The maximum height of the rails is 120ft. To the credit of the architect Robert Stephenson, and contractors McKay & Blastock, the bridge has needed no major repairs in a century-and-a-half. Regrettably, posts and wires added when the line was electrified have somewhat marred the bridge's appearance. The structure is a Grade I listed building.

Passenger branches from the ECML are described in other chapters, but two abortive schemes also deserve mention. When the NER absorbed the Blyth & Tyne in 1874, there were plans for a line between Killingworth and Craghall on the former B&T near South Gosforth. This would have provided an alternative route from Newcastle, but its value was limited since the B&T terminated at New Bridge Street - the link to Newcastle Central eventually opened in 1909.

In 1919, to reduce the congestion, particularly of goods trains in central Newcastle and on the two adjacent Tyne bridges, the NER proposed a Newcastle-avoiding line. Its northern end would join the ECML at a triangular junction close to the Coast Road. Passing through Walker (with connections to the Riverside Branch), it would cross the Tyne at St Anthony's, and join the Leamside line near Pelaw. St Anthony's Bridge was to be high level, of steel construction, and accommodate a double-track railway, a highway, and a pair of tram tracks. The layout would take rail traffic from a planned marshalling yard at Washington into Heaton Yard, onto the Riverside Branch, or to the ECML in Northumberland. Passenger trains could use the route, though few would need to bypass Newcastle. In 1922-23 the NER/LNER bought a 45-acre strip between Benfield Road and St Anthony's from Newcastle Corporation for the new route. The Corporation altered road-building plans to minimise crossings of the proposed railway. At St Anthony's a separate purchase of 8⅓ acres was negotiated with Lord Northbourne. The railway was never built, but its route could be discerned sixty years later as a stretch of allotments and open space.

The history of ECML motive power and rolling stock is amply described in other books. In 1854 the NER absorbed the YN&BR. From 1869 the NER began to operate trains over NB metals in exchange for NBR running powers between Newcastle and Hexham; a change of locomotives was no longer needed at Berwick. Intense competition with the West Coast (London Euston-Edinburgh) route encouraged ECML services to accelerate from the 1880s and, apart from the disruption caused by the two wars, speeds and frequencies have steadily improved. The ECML has enjoyed some of Britain's fastest scheduled services, such as *The Flying Scotsman* and *The Talisman*. The *Flying Scotsman* was allowed 9½ hours between the capitals in 1876 (reduced to 4h 9m by 2001). Regular weekday Newcastle-Edinburgh northbound 'inter-city' services increased from 17 in 1961 to 29 in 2000. Prestigious motive power has hauled ECML trains, notably streamlined A4 Pacifics from 1935-1961, and Class 55 (Deltic) diesels through the 1960s and 70s. From the late 1970s, Class 43 Inter-City 125s were introduced. Class 91 locomotives have been used since electrification of the route in 1991.

Local passenger trains were steam-operated until about 1960. Since then, despite electrification, dmus have provided the local service. On weekdays in summer 1950, prior to the closure of many minor stations, three trains operated each way between Newcastle and Berwick, calling at most stations, with four further Newcastle-Alnwick trains. Additional 'semi-fasts' called typically at Morpeth, Alnmouth, Chathill, Belford, and Beal. By 1965 no local Newcastle-Berwick service operated, although most of the four Newcastle-Alnwick trains called at intermediate stations. When the Alnwick branch closed in 1968, two local weekday trains continued between Newcastle and Alnmouth in each direction, and certain Newcastle-Berwick trains called at selected intermediate stations. In summer 1968 Chathill's service was reduced to two down and four up trains, and Cramlington and Pegswood had three each way. Since May 1978 the weekday Newcastle-

Morpeth service has run approximately hourly. In summer 1989 there were five all-station stopping trains from Alnmouth to Newcastle (two starting at Alnmouth) and three in the reverse direction, in addition to Newcastle-Morpeth locals. However the 1993-94 timetable showed a reduction to three southbound and two northbound between Newcastle and Alnmouth, only one each way serving Manors. Meanwhile only two southbound and one northbound train served Chathill.

North of Morpeth, Northumberland's ECML weekday 'stopping' trains are now almost extinct. In winter 2002-03 there is a morning Chathill (departing 07.17) to Newcastle commuter train, and an evening service from MetroCentre (17.00) and Newcastle (17.15) to Chathill returning to Newcastle (arriving 19.47). It is thus impractical to travel between Berwick and Chathill, but even in 1965 a BR census showed that all travel to and from Chathill was from the south.

Review of the stations

Stations between Newcastle and Berwick were numerous and closely spaced, on average only two miles apart. Almost all were the work of Benjamin Green, a Newcastle architect who, with his father, designed Newcastle's Theatre Royal and Grey's Monument. N&B stations were generally very fine, resembling each other in their Tudor/Jacobean appearance, but with different details. Hallmarks were the buff-coloured stone, prominent chimneystacks, and ball finials on gable ends. Tweedmouth and Morpeth, befitting their importance, received the largest structures. More extensive station buildings usually contained two dwellings, the larger for the stationmaster, and the smaller for a porter. Some buildings were reminiscent of manor houses, with an H-plan whose cross-wings enclosed a verandah. There were distinctive raised gables (as at Acklington). A further design (as at Chathill) had a central projection towards the platform ending with a two-storey bay, topped by a gable resting on corbels. The second dwelling here was built as a wing, creating an overall L-plan. Three smaller station buildings (Widdrington, Cragg Mill, and Scremerston) had overhanging eaves with attractive bargeboards and resembled picturesque rural cottages. Smaller still were crossing houses, as at Goswick, consisting of semi-detached dwellings with dormers. Some minor stations (e.g. Lucker) had remarkably lavish buildings, but Cramlington, exceptionally, had small, dull structures. The original Berwick station was of NBR provenance, and not designed by Green. For further architectural details of N&B stations Fawcett's *North Eastern Railway Architecture: The Pioneers* (2001) is strongly recommended.

To the original sixteen stations between Newcastle and Tweedmouth, others were added, usually alongside original crossing cottages, as at Goswick. Entirely new stations included Dudley (1860, replaced by Annitsford in 1878) and

Forest Hall, looking southeast in 1959, shortly after closure to passengers.   (Stations UK)

Lucker Troughs, with Class A1 No 60152 *Holyrood* travelling north in August 1955. *(J W Armstrong Trust)*

Pegswood (1903). Berwick station was rebuilt in 1927. Early closures were Lesbury (1851) and Ashington Colliery Junction and Cragg Mill (1877). Closure of Smeafield and Fallodon followed in the 1930s. During World War II several lightly-used stations closed to passengers in 1941, reopening in 1946: these were Longhoughton, Little Mill, Christon Bank, Newham, Lucker, Goswick, and Scremerston. From 1950 closures resumed, affecting, in quick succession, Newham (1950), Scremerston and Longhirst (1951), and Lucker (1953). A purge of King's Cross-Berwick 'roadside' stations took place in 1957-59. The Northumbrian casualties were Forest Hall, Killingworth, Annitsford, Plessey, Stannington, Chevington, Warkworth, Little Mill, Christon Bank, and Goswick, in 1958. Pegswood, considered for closure at that time, was reprieved. Longhoughton succumbed in 1962 and Tweedmouth in 1964.

In 1966 BR proposed to close Pegswood, Widdrington, Belford, and Beal, as well as Alnwick. The Secretary of State's decision was to refuse to close Pegswood and Widdrington, but permit passenger services to be withdrawn from Belford, Beal, and Alnwick; they closed in 1968. Since then Heaton has also closed (1980).

In the early 1970s, when many British stations were 'simplified', all 1847 ECML Northumbrian station buildings were spared, and electric lighting and corporate identity nameplates were installed. Until then, most stations retained LNER wooden nameboards with raised letters, latterly in corporate identity black-and-white. British Railways 'totem' nameplates appeared only at Berwick. Among the open stations Pegswood and Cramlington have had their main buildings demolished, but these were of little architectural merit. The loss of Alnmouth station's buildings was more regrettable. Between Newcastle and Berwick, only Morpeth and

Alnmouth stations are now staffed. Many disused stations' buildings survive thanks to their architectural excellence and suitability for residential use.

Station-by-station

Forest Hall opened as Benton in 1856 but was renamed in 1874 to avoid confusion with Benton (Blyth & Tyne). All buildings were at the southeast end. The station house on the up platform was originally a crossing cottage, and was later extended. It featured a projecting gable and ground-floor bay window. The down platform had a wooden ridged shelter. A standard NER iron footbridge adjoined the crossing. The signal cabin on the up platform was perched on girders above the footbridge steps. In 1924 the LNER planned to demolish the two-track station and build a new one with two island platforms, served by four tracks. A classically styled single-storey entrance building would be on a new road overbridge, south of the level crossing. Two plans were proposed, one placing the new overbridge and station facilities some 40 yd south of the other, and the two designs of entrance buildings differed in detail. Neither plan came to fruition. In 1951 tickets issued amounted to 1,928. Although in an urban area, the station was little used. Buses were frequent, and Benton station, with frequent services to Newcastle, was several minutes' walk away. Passenger closure in 1958 was followed by demolition in 1964. The *Flying Scotsman* public house now adjoins the station site.

Killingworth had a fine building on the down platform. Two-storey wings, with a verandah between them, projected at each end, and had ground floor bays. There was a further verandah at the north end. The up platform had an elegant stone shelter with an wood-and-glass front. At the level crossing, an NER footbridge connected the

KEY
- ●—— Passenger railway / station open in 1914
- +—— Other railway / untimetabled station
- ○—— Passenger station closed before 1914
- ◉—— Passenger station opened after 1914

N

To Edinburgh
BERWICKSHIRE
BERWICK
TWEEDMOUTH
VELVET HALL
SCREMERSTON
NORHAM
GOSWICK
BEAL
Holy Island (Lindisfarne)
TWIZELL
COLDSTREAM
CARHAM
SUNILAWS
SMEAFIELD
Farne Islands
SPROUSTON
MINDRUM
CRAGG MILL
KELSO
BELFORD
SEAHOUSES
ST. BOSWELLS
Rutherford
LUCKER
NORTH SUNDERLAND
Roxburgh
AKELD
NEWHAM
Maxton
KIRKNEWTON
WOOLER
CHATHILL
Falloden
Kirkbank
ILDERTON
CHRISTON BANK
Nisbet
Jedfoot
WOOPERTON
LITTLE MILL
Jedburgh
HEDGELEY
LONGHOUGHTON
ROXBURGHSHIRE
GLANTON
ALNWICK
LESBURY
Hawick
WHITTINGHAM
ALNMOUTH
EDLINGHAM
WARKWORTH
AMBLE
Catcleugh Reservoir
ROTHBURY
ACKLINGTON
BROOMHILL
SAUGHTREE
BRINKBURN
CHEVINGTON
RICCARTON JN.
DEADWATER
FONTBURN
WIDDRINGTON
DUMFRIESSHIRE
Steele Road
KIELDER FOREST
EWESLEY
LONGHIRST
ASHINGTON COLL. JN.
Ashington
LEWIEFIELD HALT
LONGWITTON
PEGSWOOD
NEWBIGGIN
Newcastleton
PLASHETTS
THORNEYBURN
MIDDLETON NORTH
MORPETH
NORTH SEATON
FALSTONE
TARSET
WOODBURN
SCOTSGAP
ANGERTON
CHOPPINGTON
BEDLINGTON
CHARLTON
Vickers Platform
Parsons Platform
KNOWESGATE
MELDON
BEBSIDE
BELLINGHAM (North Tyne)
REEDSMOUTH
STANNINGTON
HEPSCOTT
BLYTH
COUNTESS PARK
Kirkheaton Coll.
PLESSEY
NEWSHAM
Riddings Jn.
CUMBERLAND
WARK
CRAMLINGTON
HARTLEY
BARRASFORD
PONTELAND
CHOLLERTON
DARRAS HALL
GREENHEAD
FOURSTONES
HUMSHAUGH
NORTH WYLAM
GILSLAND
Blenkinsopp Hall Halt
ALLERWASH
WALL
PRUDHOE
BRAMPTON TOWN
HALTWHISTLE
HAYDON BRIDGE
WARDEN
MICKLEY
WYLAM
NEWCASTLE
LOW ROW
BARDON MILL
HEXHAM
NAWORTH
Plenmeller Halt
See enlargement of Newcastle area
BRAMPTON JN.
FEATHERSTONE PARK
ELRINGTON
CORBRIDGE
CARLISLE
Kirkhouse
COANWOOD
LANGLEY
RIDING MILL
Citadel
BRAMPTON FELL
LAMBLEY
STAWARD
STOCKSFIELD
HOW MILL
London Rd.
HEADS NOOK
SCOTBY
WETHERAL
ALLENDALE
SLAGGYFORD
CO. DURHAM
ALSTON

KEY
1 Ashington Colliery
2 New Moor
3 Linton Colliery
4 Ellington Colliery

MILES
0 ... 5 ... 10
0 ... 5 ... 10 ... 15
KILOMETRES

AEY 6/02

platforms. The station was over a mile from Killingworth and adjoined West Moor, a colliery village. In 1911 over 34,000 tickets were issued, but, from the 1920s, frequent buses and trams to Newcastle took business away. Only 1,116 passengers were booked in 1951. After passenger closure in 1958 the main line platforms were swiftly demolished, but both buildings survived into the 1970s. Three bay platforms on the down side, separate from the main station, served Gosforth Park racecourse traffic; they were used for some time after the main passenger station closed.

Annitsford opened in 1878. It replaced Dudley Colliery station which was 16 chains further north. Although in Dudley, it was named after a mining village a mile distant. The railway is on an embankment, and the main building presented a single storey to the up platform. It was brick-built with two tall forward-projecting gables enclosing a verandah. A waiting shelter and booking office on

7

the down platform faced the main building. In 1911, 49,132 tickets were issued. Bus competition eroded rail traffic, and issues fell to 2,635 in 1951. After closure in 1958 the station was soon demolished.

Dudley Colliery opened in 1860 - it was called Dudley until 1874 - and is shown on an 1879 Ordnance Survey map with buildings on both platforms. It has gone without trace.

Cramlington was one of the original stations. It had a collection of unattractive buildings on the up platform. A brick single-storey structure with a hipped roof had a recessed central section to provide shelter. Flanking it were two small brick buildings, and terraced cottages backed the remainder of the platform. A small stone shelter with a timber-and-glass front, entered from the south end, stood on the down platform. A standard NER footbridge was provided. By 1991 a new footbridge was installed, with clearance for overhead electrification. The vandalised main building lasted until about 1993. Modern shelters are now installed. Cramlington's service has improved dramatically since the late 1950s when two southbound and three northbound trains called. In

c 1900

Forest Hall. Architects' drawings of extensions to the up platform building (NER c1900) and of two possible designs for a new overbridge building spanning the proposed four-track layout (LNER 1924). The quadrupling scheme was never carried out. *(Alan Young Collection)*

PLAN A 1924

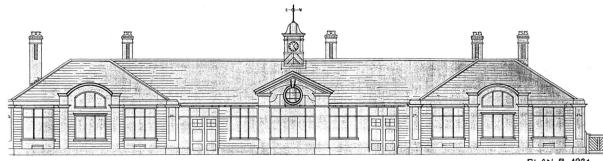

PLAN B 1924

On 1 January 1973 the stately building at Killingworth stands derelict. Racecourse traffic platforms were formerly located in the wasteland beyond the building.

(Alan Young)

Annitsford, looking south in 1958, the year of closure. The sober building on the up platform was designed by William Peachey, NER Architect 1876-77. The building had a further storey below platform level.

(Stations UK)

At Cramlington the original passenger facilities were a temporary wooden building and a waiting shed. In 1855 the permanent building, designed by the NER Civil Engineer, was added on the up platform. On 30 July 1991 a Newcastle - Morpeth dmu No 143 622 calls.

(Alan Young)

the 1960s Cramlington village was expanded into a new town. Traffic potential increased enormously, although the station is far from the town centre. The 4,195 tickets issued in 1951 grew to 23,470 in 1972. In recent years between ten and twelve weekday trains in each direction have called.

Plessey's building resembled that at Forest Hall. It stood on the down platform near the level crossing, accompanied by a pent-roofed timber shed. The down platform had a small waiting shed. The main structure (1847) was a crossing cottage, but platforms were installed permitting market trains to call. In 1859 Plessey became a public station. In the mid-1860s *Bradshaw* rendered the name as Plessy; the working timetable called it Plessay. This rural station (which issued only 2,376 tickets in 1936) was unstaffed from 8 July 1951,

when four weekday trains called in each direction. From September 1955 until closure in 1958, Plessey's solitary passenger train departure was northbound at 7.50 am on weekdays. The station has been demolished.

Stannington, opened as Netherton, was renamed in 1892 after a village almost two miles away. An L-plan Benjamin Green building of substantial size survives beside the up line. It has a corbelled-out gable with two-storey bay, and a verandah on the north side. In 1951 Stannington issued only 527 tickets. It closed in 1958.

Morpeth is served by some long-distance trains and is the terminus of a frequent service to Newcastle. Passenger bookings of 9,700 in 1951 increased to 25,097 in 1972. There are two main line platforms. From 1880 a bay at the north end of the

Plessey, looking southeast in the NER era.
(Alan Young Collection)

On 27 August 1974 the 14.00 London King's Cross - Edinburgh Waverley, hauled by Deltic No 55 016 *Gordon Highlander,* passes Stannington
(Tom Heavyside)

The exterior of Morpeth main line station in August 2001. It has been little altered since its construction in 1847. Recent cleaning allows the quality of the masonry to be enjoyed to the full.　*(Alan Young)*

up platform accommodated ex-Blyth & Tyne trains. The down platform was an island, the outer line used by the NBR. A subway connected the platforms. The main building, a fine, rock-faced stone structure with ashlar quoins, is on the up platform. Booking and parcel facilities were in a wooden edifice at right-angles to the main building. A generous slate-covered awning sheltered much of the platform. The island platform had an iron and glass umbrella awning, resting on two lines of columns. Both awnings featured Star of David spandrels, a design favoured by the NER in the 1880s. The main building remains, but its tall chimneystacks have been shortened. The up platform awnings are reduced to a token remnant fronting the main building. The island awning was dismantled following damage caused by a derailment in 1969. An NER system tile map, dating from about 1905, is still displayed.

Pegswood was added in 1903 to serve a colliery village. Compared with its neighbours, it was a poor relation. The main building was an austere structure on an over-bridge. Each platform had a ridged-roof brick building containing waiting rooms and toilets. With a paltry service of two northbound and one southbound on Mondays to Fridays (and a marginally better Saturday service) in 1958 Pegswood was considered for closure, but survived. Ten years later it again escaped closure. It is unclear from the TUCC Report of 1966 why the fifteen passengers (six 'regulars') using Pegswood retained their service. In the 1970s/80s departures ranged from three to five each way on weekdays, and bookings amounted to only 3,388 in 1972. The station degenerated into a derelict, overgrown mess. Its entrance building was demolished, and for some years the platforms were unlit. By 1977 electric lighting was installed. Eventually the remaining building, on the up platform, was dismantled and

replaced with a 'bus shelter', and the platform surfaces were upgraded. There is no shelter for any passengers awaiting the one northbound stopping train that calls on weekdays.

Ashington Colliery Junction appeared as a column note in timetables from December 1871 until August 1878. Ordnance Survey plans of 1859 and 1897 show a building on the site, without road access, between the ECML and the mineral line to Ashington. In May 1877 only the Saturday 3.30 pm from Newcastle to Tweedmouth called.

Longhirst was another station with an imposing building, this time on the down platform. The structure contained two houses, each having a gable-end facing the platform, the northern one slightly projecting and with a two-storey bay. A verandah was enclosed in the central recess. The station closed in 1951, but the building remains intact.

Widdrington's building is of the smaller cottage style (similar to Scremerston) on the up platform. A single gable faces the platform, with a single-storey bay. A wood-and-glass waiting room formerly adjoined on the north side. Raising of the platform height has partly obscured the ground floor of the building. A brick-and-timber signal box stood at the north end of the up platform but was removed by 1992. Unlike many stations, Widdrington's business increased from 2,751 ticket issues in 1951, to 7,901 in 1967. In 1966, when the Transport Users' Consultative Committee considered BR's intention to close the station, 35 daily (thirteen regular) passengers were identified. The case against closure was aided by plans for 105 houses to be built beside the station, and by the local authority's determination to attract employment after the recent closure of the local colliery. The station was retained, and, in 1972, 12,695 tickets were issued, reflecting local population growth and an improved service.

Morpeth, looking northeast along the island platform in 1963. North British trains to Rothbury formerly used the left side of this platform.
(Stations UK)

On 6 April 1977 a Class 37 diesel hauls a southbound coal train through Pegswood. The station offices on the overbridge had been removed by this time, leaving only the building on the up platform; this, too, would soon disappear. *(Alan Young)*

Widdrington, looking north in April 1979. The modest cottage contrasts with the more extravagant buildings at some of the other original Newcastle & Berwick Railway stations. *(Alan Young)*

The down main line platform at Chevington, with an Amble branch passenger train in the bay. The photograph was taken from the up platform.
(Alan Young Collection)

Acklington, seen from a southbound train on 12 April 1966. The splendid neo-Tudor building is accompanied by an LNER nameboard, an NER gradient post and oil lanterns.
(Geoffrey C Lewthwaite)

Warkworth, looking south from the down platform in NER days. Today the fine station building is in residential use, but the platforms have been removed.
(Alan Young Collection)

However it now shares Pegswood's minimal train service.

Chevington possessed only a crossing cottage in 1847. Despite its remote location, a passenger station opened in 1870, served initially by four weekday and two Sunday trains each way. It had staggered platforms, the down platform displaced northwards. In 1879 it became the terminus for Amble branch passenger trains, which (until withdrawn in 1930) used a down side bay platform, where passenger facilities were contained in a dull, single-storey brick building. Latterly little passenger traffic was handled - 982 tickets were issued in 1951. It closed in 1958.

Acklington station opened with the line. The main building (down platform) consists of two wings with raised gables, the booking and parcels office in the north wing having a bay window. A verandah, supported by branched wooden posts, stretches between the wings and fronts the former general waiting room. The northward end's high roof sweeps down to cover another verandah, behind which were the booking hall and first class waiting rooms. The south wing ground floor and the upper storey provided housing for the stationmaster and a porter, the former enjoying more generous provision. The up platform's waiting shed is a lengthy structure with pent-roof and stone end- and back-walls. The front has herringbone timberwork to dado level, over thirty small windows, and a central entrance. Complementing the passenger station, the stone-built goods shed is splendid, unashamedly Gothic, and with a pointed arch that allowed rail access. Happily the buildings survive in good condition.

The station is a short distance from Acklington village. It formerly served an RAF base, thus some express trains stopped; in summer 1954 the 12.55 am King's Cross to Edinburgh called at 7.23 am (Monday only) for personnel returning from weekend leave. In 1966, whilst Pegswood (population 2,590) and Widdrington (population 4,400) were proposed for closure, BR explained that Acklington (population 406) would remain open because, unlike its neighbours, it handled a significant amount of long-distance traffic. (A traffic census in July 1965 showed an average of 43 daily users of Acklington, but 68 of Widdrington.) The RAF establishment has closed, and traffic has dwindled. Ticket sales fell from 4,513 in 1967 to 2,464 in 1972. It remains open with a limited commuter service.

Warkworth station was 1½ miles from the delightful village beside the River Coquet, dominated by a ruined castle, and 3 miles from Amble. On the site of the up platform, which adjoined a level crossing, is a stately building of three storeys, the upper two facing the rails. It is one of the larger designs, consisting of end wings, a two-storey bay window, and a verandah between the wings. The exterior has a small portico, approached by a flight of steps. The down platform, staggered northwards, was connected to the up platform by a barrow crossing and a passenger subway. The inconvenient location limited the station's

The main line platforms at Alnmouth, looking north, with 4-4-0 No 723. *(Alan Young Collection)*

Lesbury station was open from 1847 until 1851 and served Alnwick. The station building was still in residential use, when photographed on 27 February 1953.
(J W Armstrong, courtesy Ken Hoole Study Centre, Darlington)

Longhoughton, looking south from the down platform in 1959.
(John F Mallon, courtesy Ken Hoole Study Centre, Darlington)

Little Mill. The subsidiary building with its unusual awning, on the up platform.
(John F Mallon, courtesy Ken Hoole Study Centre, Darlington)

usefulness, but immediately prior to closure there was a more generous train service than was enjoyed by the other 1958 casualties. The main building remains in residential use.

South of Warkworth a branch some four miles in length served Whittle Colliery, but it closed in 1987. Another two-mile branch north of Warkworth served Shilbottle Colliery, which closed in 1982.

Alnmouth (Bilton until 2 May 1892) opened in October 1850 with the Alnwick branch. Benjamin Green designed the station on a tighter budget than earlier ECML buildings. The station was replaced in 1886-87, but the original building was retained, adjacent to the new structures designed by the NER Architect, William Bell. The new station received partially glazed awnings on the up platform (where the main facilities were located) and on the island platform that served the down main line and Alnwick branch. The awnings were ridged on the up platform, but hipped on the island. Corinthian pillars and spandrels with a quatrefoil decoration supported the awnings, and there were glazed end-screens. A narrow, enclosed footbridge connected the platforms. Before modernisation in the early 1970s the character of Alnmouth station was more urban than rural, reminiscent of Blaydon. By 1972 the island platform lost its building and awning, and a brick shelter was installed. The modest LNER electric lamps (and name tablets) were removed and replaced with tall vandal-proof posts. In 1977 the platforms were raised to standard height. The up platform buildings were replaced in 1987 with a neat brick building possessing a low, pitched roof and overhanging eaves. It contained booking, parcels and waiting facilities. An NER signal box is the only significant historic structure to survive the alterations.

Ticket issues at Alnmouth stood at 49,041 in 1911 and 15,158 in 1951. Its importance has declined, with closure of its locomotive shed in 1966 and withdrawal of Alnwick trains in 1968. It now serves as the railhead for Alnwick, from which some business is derived; ticket sales of 14,071 in 1967 rose to 17,752 in 1972, following Alnwick's closure, but the increase fell far short of the number of passengers who could have been booked if Alnwick's 15,138 bookings (1967) had been inherited. In addition to Newcastle-Chathill locals, several long-distance services call, including Glasgow-London expresses.

Lesbury survived until 1851, serving Alnwick. The station house (now demolished) was on the down side, south of the bridge on the Lesbury-Alnwick road. It featured the familiar raised gables and ground-floor bay windows.

Longhoughton was adjacent to the village, and latterly served an airfield. It was one of the original stations with a 'line style' building, adapted to its position on an embankment. The upper of the two storeys faced the platform, and a bay window and verandah fronted the structure. The main facilities were on the up side. A lengthy waiting shed stood

on the down platform, and a signal box at the north end. The needs of RAF personnel explain timetable oddities. For example in winter 1961-62 the Monday-only Glasgow-York service called at 1.51 am and at Acklington (again to serve an RAF base) at 2.4 am, with no other calls between Berwick and Newcastle. Despite its convenient situation the station was lightly used, only 159 tickets being sold in 1951. Nevertheless services continued until 1962. The platforms and other structures were demolished shortly after closure.

Little Mill station was provided to appease the landowner, Earl Grey of Howick. Though originally private, in 1861 a public service began. Both platforms were north of the level crossing. The down platform house had raised gables, ball finials and tall chimneys. At the southern end a single-storey wing with south-facing bay contained a private waiting room; this eventually became a public first-class facility. An awning stretched along the exterior and platform faces of this waiting room. In 1882 an upper storey was added. A third-class waiting room was in a lean-to shelter against the yard wall. If Earl Grey wished to join a southbound train, it called at this platform, with its superior waiting facilities. Queen Victoria was the most distinguished passenger. She alighted on 27 September 1849 to stay overnight at Howick Hall. The following day she continued her progress to Newcastle to open the High Level Bridge.

On the up platform stood an austere single storey stone building with a pitched roof. In its extended form it included a booking office, waiting room, ladies' room, and goods store. In front a curious open waiting shelter was constructed, notable for huge wooden brackets and glazed end-screens that supported the roof.

Business was light: in 1951 only 519 tickets were sold. Before passenger services ended in 1958, only two trains called in each direction on weekdays. The buildings and platforms were swiftly demolished.

Christon Bank station, a mile from Embleton village, was named after a nearby hamlet. It opened with the line in 1847. The commodious main building on the up platform and the Gothic goods shed - both currently used as houses - resemble structures at Acklington, with minor differences in detail. In 1951 the station issued only 440 tickets. It closed in 1958.

Fallodon was constructed for Sir George Grey of Fallodon Hall, through whose land the railway passed. It was a complete station, with two 127yd platforms north of the level crossing. The station house (down platform) had N&B hallmarks and resembled that at Little Mill. Built on an L-plan, it possessed ground floor bays, one facing the platform, the other (containing the booking office) facing the level crossing, and a small verandah. An upper storey was added to the north end in 1906. On the up platform was a pent-roof stone shelter. Like the station house, the shelter carried ball finials. A gate cabin stood south of the crossing on the down side.

Christon Bank in February 2001. Over forty years after closure the station building makes a fine private residence.
(Alan Young)

The private Fallodon station, looking north in 1959. It closed following the death in 1933 of Viscount Grey of Fallodon, Director of the LNER and former Foreign Secretary (1905-16).
(Stations UK)

Unlike Little Mill, Fallodon remained private for Sir George and his family, guests, and servants. Nevertheless, NER nameboards were installed. The favoured few could request any passenger train to call. Conditions of use permitted 'taking up and landing of passengers' as well as the handling of 'carriages and trucks with coals and other goods'. These rights extended to heirs to his property. The station was a drain on NER finances: in 1914 only eighteen passengers were booked! When the Fallodon estate passed to Capt. & Mrs Graves, the LNER obtained the couple's consent in 1934 to cancel their right to stop trains, in return for an all stations LNER pass for life. Trains ceased to call in 1935, but the platforms and buildings survived until about 1960.

Chathill station stands in lonely countryside, with a few houses huddled beside it. No main line trains call, but two *Arriva* local diesel services to and from Newcastle terminate here - are there any more unlikely termini in Britain? The few passengers can admire the features that justify its Grade II listed status: the elegant main building; a waiting shed with a quirkily sagging roof; and an oil lantern cradle. Chathill (Chat-hill in early publications) opened in March 1847. On the down platform, the main building has a projecting central section with a two-storey bay corbelled out to support a gable, decorated with a blind arch. Research by W. Fawcett has revealed that there were originally verandahs

either side of the central gable, but when a waiting room was added to the south, the northern verandah was removed and the southern one was lengthened. These NER additions were executed sensitively; even the wooden branching columns supporting the verandah almost exactly matched the original ones.

From 1898 until 1951 Chathill was the junction for Seahouses. Branch trains used a bay behind the up platform. Until 1965 there were goods facilities, handling coal, barley, fish, and timber. Despite passenger bookings of only 3,221 in 1951, falling to 1,693 in 1972, Chathill survived the 1950s purge of stations. It served the local post office delivery centre, and was railhead for a large catchment area. When, in 1966, Belford's closure was proposed, several objectors were perplexed by the threat to Belford (population 891) while Chathill (population 50) was to stay open. One correspondent asked, 'Why should Chathill have preferential immunity?' A Bamburgh hotelier believed 'Belford is 100% more convenient for Belford, Bamburgh and Seahouses', whilst other local residents claimed that bus connections to Chathill were 'almost useless', and that if a station had to be closed it should be Chathill. BR justified its decision since - inaccessible or not - Chathill handled twice as many passengers as Belford. (BR's census in July 1965 actually showed a weekday average of eleven passengers using Chathill and ten using Belford!)

On 17 April 1979 the 14.00 London King's Cross - Edinburgh Waverley, hauled by Deltic No 55 018 *Ballymoss*, hurtles through Chathill station. *(Alan Young)*

Newham, shortly before World War I. Station gardens were often carefully tended; this one on the down platform, featuring the NER motif, was a fine example
(Alan Young Collection)

Lucker, looking north in 1958, five years after closure. This minor station boasted a particularly large and elaborate building.
(Stations UK)

Cragg Mill's passenger service lasted from 1871 until 1877, but its building remained intact long after closure.
(Courtesy Ken Hoole Study Centre, Darlington)

In the late-1970s the station was a remarkable relic. Deltic-hauled expresses and Inter-City 125s sped past the Victorian buildings, the row of oil lamps, and the LNER nameboards still proclaiming 'Chathill for Seahouses'. In the 1980s, installation of electric lighting, followed by the wires and ironmongery of the electrification scheme, and the removal of the footbridge, greatly altered the station's character.

Newham possessed only a crossing cottage in 1847. From 1851 passenger facilities were available. The platforms were staggered either side of the crossing. The cottage (Chevington type) was on the the down platform south of the crossing, accompanied by a later station house of simple design. Traffic was light; even in 1911 fewer than ten tickets were sold each day, allowing time for the staff to maintain a splendid garden. The station closed in 1950, and the two weekday trains in each direction ceased to call. The platforms were demolished, but the buildings survived into the 1970s. A new cottage now stands on the site.

Lucker was noted for its troughs, installed in 1898 south of the station, enabling locomotives to take up water without stopping. This minor station received a remarkably large, elaborate building, combining wings (as at Warkworth) and projecting central section with two-storey bays (as at Chathill). A small, stone shelter stood on the opposite (up) platform. Passenger bookings (277 in 1951) were insufficient to justify the one southbound and two northbound departures, which ceased in 1953. Regrettably the station was demolished in 1960.

Belford has a substantial building on the down side. The platform elevation consists of two wings, the southern one with a two-storey bay. Between them is a verandah with timber and glazed front. Single storey sections complete the building at the north and south ends. A further verandah fronts the southern section. The frontage has a buttressed portico with lancet arches. The up platform (now demolished) had a stone, wood, and glass shelter. A typical NER iron footbridge connected the platforms. Between the up platform and level crossing were a water crane and a gantry-mounted signal box. The box was replaced in the 1960s with a bland structure - now disused and partly demolished - on the opposite side of the line.

Neither Belford nor Beal were proposed for closure by Beeching. Nevertheless, withdrawal of passenger services was published on 3 March 1966 and approved on 28 September 1967. During 1967 Belford's passenger bookings totalled 1,346. That autumn, passenger train departures amounted to two on Monday-Friday, and three on Saturday northbound, with three southbound on weekdays. Belford's closure was passionately resisted. Typically, ten passengers used the station on weekdays, rising to 25 on summer Saturdays, but only four *regular* users were identified. Closure was implemented in 1968. The main building (Grade II listed) survives in residential use, part let as a holiday cottage. North of the station, sidings continue to serve a quarry. Pressure to reopen Belford station has recently grown as local residents have noted that Newcastle-Chathill trains actually operate to Belford in order to cross from the down to the up track.

Cragg Mill was open from February 1871 until September 1877, and its service was limited to Tuesdays and Saturdays. Curiously, the contract for Newcastle & Berwick buildings makes no reference to Cragg Mill, even as a crossing cottage, yet the station possessed a building resembling those at Scremerston and Widdrington. It was a charming design including elaborate bargeboards with ball pendants. A goods siding and coal depot outlived the passenger station, and the station building probably survived into the 1970s.

Smeafield, like Cragg Mill, opened to passengers in 1871 and had a meagre train service. The cottage, dating from 1847, stands on the down side, north of the level crossing. Its design was similar to Forest Hall's building. Platforms were added later, also north of the crossing. An unadvertised passenger service probably operated before public opening. *Bradshaw* (1910) showed several trains calling by request on Monday, Tuesday, and Saturday. Passengers were few; in 1911 only 35 people were within the station's catchment, and only 369 tickets were issued. In 1930 Smeafield closed, but for some time trains continued to make unadvertised calls. The cottage is in residential use.

Beal served five generations of pilgrims and holidaymakers to Holy Island (Lindisfarne). Bradley in *Romance of Northumberland* (1908) recollects

On 23 October 1967 the York to Edinburgh Waverley train calls at Belford at 10.11 to discharge one passenger and collect parcels. *(Alan Young)*

Smeafield station did little business and closed in 1930. This view dates from 1958.
(Stations UK)

arriving at Beal by train where, since the tide was out and the causeway passable, horse-drawn carts awaited hire for the treacherous journey to the island. On the down platform the building, as at Longhirst, consisted of a pair of two-storey blocks joined by a single storey section with a tall roof; this contained waiting accommodation and a verandah. On the up platform was a shed with a timber-and-glass front.

In 1967 only 201 tickets were sold (down from 1,677 in 1951) and its train departures were two northbound on Monday-Friday (three on Saturday) and two southbound on weekdays. In 1966 BR proposed closure. Their census discovered no regular passengers, and only six-to-twelve daily users, some of whom used Holiday Runabout tickets so did not contribute to the statistics of tickets issued at the station. BR dismissed claims that Holy Island's tourist trade would suffer, noting how few passengers used the station, and recommending the use of taxis from the mainland. In October 1967, when I visited Beal station, it was in immaculate condition. The platforms appeared to have recently been tarmaced. The stone edging of the garden was whitened, and the shrubs trimmed. The oil lanterns were painted in oriental blue, and the LNER 'Beal for Holy Island' nameboard was resplendent in NE Region orange. A few weeks later, in January 1968, it closed to all traffic. In 1979 the fine main building was demolished.

Goswick was in a tranquil landscape where a winding lane met the coastal dunes. The station served Goswick and Windmill Hill farms, and a golf course. In 1847 a crossing cottage, resembling Lesbury station house, was constructed. The station first appeared in *Bradshaw* of November 1870 as Wind Mill Hall, corrected in December to Wind Mill Hill. At first it was a request stop for three weekday and two Sunday trains in each direction. In 1898 the name was changed to Goswick. The layout resembled some York-Scarborough line stations

with platforms staggered either side of the crossing (down platform to the south) and the original cottage, north of the crossing, was not at a platform. The up platform had a small stone-built ticket office and waiting room, while the up platform possessed a timber waiting room.

From 1952 until closure in 1958, Goswick had a strangely unbalanced timetable. Northbound trains called at 9.48 am (weekdays), 6.15 pm (Monday-Friday) and 7.1 pm (Saturday), with just one southbound departure on Thursday (12.4 pm) and Saturday (1.25 pm). This service allowed a Saturday morning visit to Berwick market; a couple of hours' shopping in Newcastle on Thursday or Saturday; or a more leisurely afternoon visit to Alnwick (changing at Alnmouth), on Thursday, or on Saturday if they were prepared to wait almost two hours for their connection at Alnmouth! The platforms and passenger buildings have long been demolished, but the cottage and down platform's back-wall survive.

Scremerston was an isolated station, over a mile from its village. The platforms were immediately north of the level crossing. The building (up platform) survives and is of the Widdrington style. By winter 1950/51 only the 10.4 am and northbound 5.4 pm southbound trains called, a service suited to a day's shopping in Berwick. Early in 1951 a review disclosed that in 1950 only £5.00 was taken in fares - equivalent to one 3rd Class monthly return to London! Goods receipts were small, and parcels traffic was minimal. Closure followed in July 1951. Before World War II a colliery at Scremerston was connected to the main line by a two-mile branch.

Tweedmouth was the northern ECML terminus from March 1847 until August 1850, when the Royal Border Bridge opened. Passengers for Berwick were conveyed by road vehicles. Temporary wooden buildings sufficed for the first year, before a splendid permanent station opened, designed by Benjamin Green. Tweedmouth was never intended to remain a terminus, and its importance would be limited to

Beal was the gateway to Holy Island. This 1958 view of A3 4-6-2 No 60076 *Galopin*, travelling north, shows the commodious building
(Stations UK)

Goswick station, opened in 1870, incorporated the existing crossing house and was provided with the rudimentary buildings seen in this view in 1958, the year of closure. *(Stations UK)*

Scremerston, looking south, in 1958. The station closed to all traffic seven years earlier, and the platforms are being demolished. Note the stone construction of the signal box.
(Stations UK)

serving as junction for the Kelso branch. Nevertheless, George Hudson marked the boundary of his railway kingdom in style. The permanent station possessed a lengthy, tall single-storey structure on the down platform. The façade's centrepiece was a five-arched entrance surmounted by Dutch gables. At the northern end was a two-storey hotel, lavishly decorated with Dutch gables, tall chimneys, and bay windows with deep parapets. Four running lines separated the platforms, which, until about 1907, were covered by a trainshed. This had twin pitched roofs, one supported by a wall behind the up platform, the other by the main building, and both rested on columns midway between the platforms. When the trainshed was removed, glazed awnings were installed over both platforms, with end-screens provided, except at the down south end. A subway connected the platforms. From 1847 Tweedmouth had a locomotive shed, stabling over 50 engines in the 1920s. It declined with dieselisation and closed in 1966.

Although Tweedmouth was among the largest population centres on the ECML in Northumberland (approximately 4,000) Berwick eclipsed it in importance. In 1951 only 1,957 tickets were issued. By summer 1960 one 'local' passenger train in each direction called at Tweedmouth on weekdays, the poorest service of any Newcastle - Berwick station. In addition, two branch trains to and from Kelso called, reversing at Tweedmouth. The station closed, with the Kelso branch, in 1964, and was soon demolished. Today it is difficult to imagine that a large station, loco shed and extensive sidings occupied the site, and that a goods branch once connected the station to Tweedmouth Dock.

Berwick-upon-Tweed (Berwick until 1955). In 1843 the NBR swept away what remained of Berwick's 12th Century castle, and drove their railway from Edinburgh through the site of the Great Hall. The station they provided - perhaps as a gesture of remorse for their vandalism! - resembled a fortress. Stone salvaged from the castle was incorporated into its structure. Massive, crenellated towers were built to conceal the arched trainshed. These were pierced by lancet windows, and, for good measure, the circular tallest tower had an additional turret. The entrance had a pointed arch, with its own set of crenellations. Two running lines and flanking platforms were beneath the trainshed. Services to Edinburgh were introduced on 22 June 1846, and the southward link across the Royal Border Bridge opened in August 1850.

In 1927 the LNER entirely rebuilt the station, installing a single island platform and a traditional awning. The two-storey entrance and office block was detached from the platform. Built of Dumfriesshire red sandstone, it was of classical design with a centrally placed clock and an iron-railed parapet. The building is Grade II listed. In the BR era, a clumsy deep valance on the entrance canopy ruined the facade. This is a busy station, the railhead for Tweedsdale and north Northumberland, with over thirty weekday train departures. 30,896 tickets were issued in 1951, rising to 48,168 in 1972.

Southbound A1 4-6-2 No 60153 *Flamboyant* uses the central track at Tweedmouth.
(Courtesy Ken Hoole Study Centre, Darlington)

The magnificent building at Tweedmouth stands empty and vandalised in this early-1960s view. The section in the foreground, resplendent with bay windows, Dutch gables and soaring chimneys, was formerly an hotel.
(Ken Hoole, courtesy Ken Hoole Study Centre, Darlington)

Berwick station in the 1860s. This remarkable castellated station building, provided by the North British Railway, was replaced with a more modest structure by the LNER in 1927.
(Courtesy Ken Hoole Study Centre, Darlington)

The original Berwick station, with flanking platforms and trainshed, is shown here in Edwardian times.
(Courtesy Ken Hoole Study Centre, Darlington)

Tweedmouth Motive Power Depot, with four K3s and a V2, on 9 July 1961.

(John Holroyd)

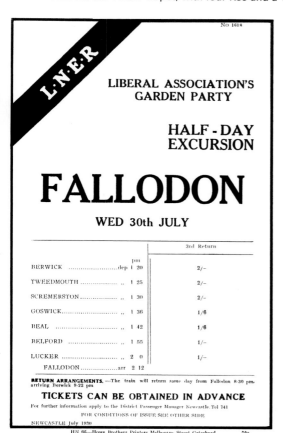

L·N·E·R

No 1618

LIBERAL ASSOCIATION'S GARDEN PARTY

HALF-DAY EXCURSION

FALLODON

WED 30th JULY

	pm	3rd Return
BERWICK ....dep	1 20	2/-
TWEEDMOUTH .... ,,	1 25	2/-
SCREMERSTON .... ,,	1 30	2/-
GOSWICK..................... ,,	1 36	1/6
BEAL .... ,,	1 42	1/6
BELFORD .... ,,	1 55	1/-
LUCKER .... ,,	2 0	1/-
FALLODON ....arr	2 12	

RETURN ARRANGEMENTS.—The train will return same day from Fallodon 8·30 pm, arriving Berwick 9·22 pm

TICKETS CAN BE OBTAINED IN ADVANCE

For further information apply to the District Passenger Manager Newcastle. Tel 741

FOR CONDITIONS OF ISSUE SEE OTHER SIDE

NEWCASTLE July 1930

H.N 65—Howe Brothers Printers Melbourne Street Gateshead   750

L·N·E·R

Glanton Flower Show.

CHEAP TICKETS

WILL BE ISSUED TO

GLANTON

On SATURDAY, 30th AUGUST, 1924

AS SHEWN BELOW.

FROM	Times of Starting		Return Fares, Third Class	Times of Return
	a.m.	a.m.		
Tweedmouth	6 8	8 44	4/7	
Velvet Hall	6 16	8 52	4/1	
Norham	6 22	8 58	3/9	
Twizell	6 28	9 3	3/5	p.m.
Coldstream	6 38	10 40	3/-	7 13
Mindrum	6 47	10 49	2/7	
Kirknewton	6 56	10 58	2/-	
Akeld	7 2	11 4	1/8	
Wooler	7 10	11 14	1/4	
Ilderton	7 19	11 23	1/-	
		p.m.		
Newcastle	6 12	12 23	6/2	
Almmouth	7 33	1 25	1/10	p.m.
Alnwick	8 27	1 50	1/6	5 29

Children not exceeding 3 years of age, free ; above 3 and under 12 years of age, half fare.

NO LUGGAGE ALLOWED.

The tickets are issued subject to the general conditions and regulations specified in the Company's current time tables ; they are available for the day of issue only ; they are not transferable, and are available only for travelling to and from the Stations named upon them by the advertised trains. If a ticket be transferred or used for any other Station than those named on it, or for any day or train other than those for which it is available, or in a higher class of carriage, it is forfeited, and the person using it is liable to pay the full fare for the journey travelled, in addition to the sum paid for the ticket.

For further information apply to Mr. E. F. WILKINSON, District Passenger Manager, Newcastle.

H.N. 413—Howe Brothers, Printers, Melbourne Street, Gateshead.

		CHEVINGTON and AMBLE.—North Eastern.													1910
Miles	**Down.**		**Week Days.**						Miles	**Up.**		**Week Days.**			
	Central Station,	mrn	mrn	aft	1212	aft	aft	aft			mrn	mrn	aft	aft	aft	aft	aft
69	NEWCASTLE ....dep	8 10	1027	1212	1 30	2 27	4 50	6 30	8 35		Amble ....dep	8 0	1026	1218	2 13	3 15	5 13	6 45	8 30	1045
—	Chevington ....dep	9 30	1153	1 26	2 50	3 45	5 38	7 53	10 0	2½	Broomhill	8 6	1033	1225	2 20	3 22	5 20	6 52	8 37	1052
3½	Broomhill	9 38	12 1	1 34	2 58	3 53	5 51	8 1	10 8	5½	Chevington 690, 691..arr	8 15	1041	1233	2 28	3 30	5 28	7 0	8 45	
5½	Amble ....arr	9 45	12 8	1 41	3 5	4 0	5 58	8 8	1015	31½	691 NEWCASTLE (Cen.)..arr	9 12	1212	1 34	4 25	6 30	6 37	8 27	10 5	

25

The Amble Branch

Several dozen passengers, military and civilian, wait at the diminutive Broomhill station about 1910.
(Alan Young Collection)

Amble grew as a port at Warkworth Harbour (the mouth of the River Coquet) dispatching coal to London, Germany, and Scandinavia. The 5-mile branch from the East Coast main line opened for mineral traffic on 5 September 1849. The passenger service, from Chevington station (on the ECML, a mile south of the junction) first appeared in the February 1879 working timetable. The branch was almost straight, gradients nowhere exceeded 1 in 117, and few earthworks were needed. There were cuttings at Broomhill and Togston, and low embankments and bridges over two streams. From the main line to Broomhill the line was single, then double track to the terminus beyond Amble station. Branches served collieries including Broomhill, Hauxley, Radcliffe, and Bullock's Hall; the latter was connected by aerial ropeway to a siding trailing from the Amble line. A gantry-mounted signal box straddled the main line at Amble junction.

In April 1910 five trains ran each way on weekdays and eight on Saturday; an extra Saturday Amble to Broomhill service served late-night revellers. Despite the inconvenience of changing to and from main line trains at Chevington, passenger traffic was buoyant in 1911, when Amble issued 31,806 tickets and Broomhill 27,746. In the 1920s passengers switched their allegiance to buses. An internal LNER memo of May 1930 stated, 'there has been such a considerable falling off in the passenger traffic of the branch that the service is being worked at a loss. Indeed the traffic is now so small that it does not even justify the maintenance of a service by steam passenger coach'. It was expected that income lost by the railway would benefit the LNER's associated bus company, *United*. Herein lies a reminder that railway companies sometimes had a financial interest in what appeared to be their competitors. Passenger closure would save 430 train miles per week, and an F8 tank engine and train set of 260 seats would be released for other duties. Passenger services ended on 7 July 1930, but the branch continued to carry coal, livestock, and other goods. Goods traffic ceased at Broomhill on 4 May 1964, and at Amble on 14 December 1964, where parcels continued to be handled. Colliery traffic used the line until complete closure, on 6 October 1969. Tracks were lifted and Amble's staiths dismantled by 1972. Both stations have been demolished, and a road occupies the trackbed between Broomhill and Acklington Prison.

The stations

At **Broomhill** a single running line served the platform (down side) widening to two lines immediately north east of the platform. A long unadorned wooden shed contained offices and waiting rooms. The goods shed stood northeast of the passenger station. **Amble** also had one passenger platform and a drab single-storey brick building with slate roof, flanked by small sheds. A wide variety of goods was handled. Beyond the passenger station the double track continued about 500yd further to the coal staiths. East of the station there was a flat crossing with a mineral line between Radcliffe and Hauxley collieries and Warkworth Harbour.

The Alnmouth – Alnwick – Coldstream Lines

Whittingham in January 1976. Today the scene is little changed, although the building on the platform has deteriorated through neglect.
(Alan Young)

Alnmouth - Alnwick

The East Coast main line was excluded from the Duke of Northumberland's estate surrounding Alnwick Castle, thus the route avoided Alnwick. Permission for a branch to Alnwick was, however, included in the Newcastle & Berwick Railway Bill. Lesbury station served Alnwick from 1847 until the branch opened from Bilton Junction (Alnmouth) to goods on 19 August 1850 and passengers on 1 October 1850. The double-track branch of 2³/₄ miles required almost continuous earthworks, and much of it was graded at 1 in 77, rising towards Alnwick. Its terminus was south of the town centre. Like other N&B stations, it was designed by Benjamin Green, but on a tighter budget. A plain block of office buildings was accompanied by a relatively small station house with a pitched roof and a prominent gable above the front door. In 1854 four trains operated each weekday, increasing to eleven weekday and four Sunday trains by 1863.

In 1887 a branch reached Alnwick from Coldstream. That year, the existing station was replaced with a magnificent structure, north of its predecessor, on a scale to impress the Duke of Northumberland's distinguished visitors. The trainsheds strongly resembled Darlington (Bank Top), opened the same year, and also designed by William Bell, Chief Architect of the NER. One long, broad, curving island platform handled passenger trains, and the offices were north of the concourse. Twin trainsheds with pitched roofs each covered two tracks, one track serving the platform and the other for engine run-round use. Between the trainsheds a smaller roof covered the platform. Arched screens concealed the trainshed roofs, whilst an end screen sheltered most of the platform width and extended upwards to the curved end of the central roof. Like some of Bell's other stations (such as Tynemouth) the frontage was dignified, but restrained. It was embellished by a slanted glass awning above the

entrance. The LNER installed electric 'mint-imperial' lamps and small nameplates. Along with hand-painted wooden nameboards, these remained until closure.

In April 1910 some twenty trains ran each way on weekdays and seven on Sunday. Alnwick was one of the last B.R. steam-operated lines, the final working being on 17 June 1966 when a 9F 2-10-0 was used. In later years K1 2-6-0 and V1/V3 2-6-2 tanks were rostered for duties. Diesel multiple units, which ultimately operated all passenger services, had been used for the Newcastle-Alnwick run and some Alnmouth 'shuttles' since 1958.

Although Beeching (1963) did not recommend closure, economies were effected by singling and re-signalling the line, and a closure proposal was published in March 1966. Alnwick and Glendale councils opposed closure on various grounds. They considered it irrational that the agricultural, educational, and cultural centre of mid-Northumberland, where tourism was being promoted, should lose its rail link. Local government offices were expanding, a 30% population increase was projected by 1980, and Development Area status was pending, to assist attempts to attract industry. The councils noted that commuting to Newcastle was increasing. (Alnwick's ticket issues rose from 7,683 in 1951 to 15,183 in 1967.)

Passenger services were withdrawn in January 1968. Users of Alnwick station (reckoned at 40-90 per day) now had to reach Alnmouth to catch trains - possibly using the bus link provided - or simply travel by car. B.R. assured objectors in 1966 that goods services would continue, but they ceased in October 1968, and the tracks were soon removed. Thankfully the fine station at Alnwick was not demolished. Much of it is now a secondhand bookshop. Pressure to reopen the line has risen, and there are plans to restore what will be known as the Aln Valley Railway.

Alnwick - Coldstream

The market town of Wooler is at the foot of the Cheviots, midway between the Aln and Tweed valleys. In 1861 the North British Railway proposed to build the Northumberland Central Railway northward to Wooler. This was to extend from the company's newly approved Wansbeck Railway at Scotsgap, reaching Wooler via Rothbury, Thropton, Alnham, and Glanton. The NCR received Royal Assent in 1862, and the Scotsgap to Rothbury section opened in 1870. However the NBR decided in 1867 to abandon the Wooler project; this was influenced by Alnwick businessmen who feared losing some of their trade to Wooler. In 1881 a Central Northumberland Railway was proposed from Newcastle to Scotsgap via Ponteland and Belsay, and from Rothbury to Wooler following a similar route to the 1861 scheme. Again this was unacceptable to Alnwick's commercial interests. An alternative NER proposal (also 1881) to connect Wooler with Alnwick and Coldstream was favoured by Parliament. In 1882 this latter route was approved. The construction contract was awarded to Meakin & Dean for what would be known as the Alnwick & Cornhill line (although Cornhill station had been renamed Coldstream in 1873).

Goods services began from Coldstream to Wooperton on 2 May 1887. The complete 35-mile Coldstream-Alnwick route opened fully on 5 September 1887, together with Alnwick's new station. The delay in completing the southern section was caused by engineering difficulties related to the curious choice of route. This railway logically should have followed a gently graded, fairly direct path of some eight miles up the Aln valley from Alnwick to Glanton. Instead it pursued a difficult course over Alnwick Moor, negotiating tight curves with almost continuous gradients of 1 in 50, on both approaches to the highest point (655ft) at Summit Cottages. At Edlingham a horseshoe curve included a five-arch viaduct. Beyond lay another ridge, requiring a 351yd tunnel at Hillhead. The route was chosen to avoid the ducal estate surrounding Alnwick Castle. In a Parliamentary Select Committee hearing of the rival NBR and NER proposals, a witness considered Alnwick-Whittingham potentially 'the worst piece of line in Northumberland, both as regards its junction with Alnwick station, the gradients, the curves ... and upon that portion of line, about a fifth of the whole length, there can be no local traffic'. After these physical challenges, the route descended to the valley of the rivers Breamish, Till, and Bowmont, which offered an easy route to Coldstream. From Bridge of Aln (Whittingham) to Akeld the railway accompanied the Morpeth-Coldstream road (A697). North of Whittingham the only significant engineering works were a deep cutting at Canno (between Kirknewton and Mindrum) and a large embankment at East Learmouth, about a mile from Coldstream station.

The passenger train service was meagre. Three each way on weekdays, stopping at all stations, and four on Saturday were adequate for this lightly populated area. No trains ran on Sunday. Around 1910 a push-and-pull Steam Autocar (a BTP tank engine and two or three coaches) operated. In LNER days G5, D17 and D20 class locomotives, were used, based at Alnmouth and Tweedmouth.The branch served a landscape of hamlets and scattered farms. Wooler, the largest intermediate settlement, had only 2,000 inhabitants. Most of the villages nominally served by the stations were some distance from the railway. Several stations were beside the A697 and particularly vulnerable to bus competition. An internal LNER memo of June 1930 noted that passenger traffic had suffered a large decline 'due, for the most part, to road competition'. Allan & Henderson and *Western* buses provided eight weekday, ten Saturday, and even three Sunday services each way between Alnwick and Wooler. *Western* buses stopped in Whittingham village, saving the inhabitants a half-hour walk to the station. *United* (an LNER associated company) provided direct Wooler-Newcastle buses - far more convenient than a train journey, changing at Alnwick and Alnmouth! Thus after only 43 years, passenger trains were withdrawn in September 1930. At the time, this was the longest British route to have closed.

Passenger trains occasionally visited the line after closure. Camping coaches were available at some stations. Holidaymakers travelled to them in a passenger coach attached to the parcels train. In World War II RAF Milfield, near Wooler, generated some traffic, and there were troop train workings. On one occasion during the war an explosion near Belford disrupted main line traffic, and a northbound express was diverted via Wooler. Goods services continued into the 1950s, generally treating the line as two branches north and south of Wooler. On 12 August 1948 storms caused severe flooding in the Borders. Considerable damage was caused to railways, and the Alnwick-Coldstream route suffered in several places. Most damage was repaired, except for a bridge between Mindrum and Kirknewton, so goods services were restored north and south of the respective stations. In October 1949 floods severed the line between Ilderton and Wooler. It was then decided to mend the bridge near Kirknewton and operate two branches: Wooler-Coldstream and Alnwick-Ilderton. The latter branch closed to all traffic in 1953, but Wooler's goods service survived until 1965.

Stations

Seventy years after closure to passengers all ten stations are well preserved. Many bridges and Edlingham Viaduct are intact. The remarkable survival rate of the stations reflects the quality of their buildings, which is unsurpassed on any other minor rural line in Britain. The stationmasters had some of the finest residences in this part of Northumberland, perhaps as recompense for being sent to such a remote area! The buildings had buff

Alnwick in June 1966. Class K1 No 62011 is running round its train before taking the next working back to Alnmouth.

(Verdun Wake / J W Armstrong Trust Collection)

coloured rock-faced sandstone walls, with slate roofs, and were of a consistent architectural style, but with interesting variations. Seven stations had two-storey houses with attached one-storey blocks containing passenger facilities. Roofs were half-hipped, with tall chimneystacks and iron finials. Single-storey versions appeared at two stations. Passengers were sheltered by herringbone patterned wood-and-glass structures that stretched along the platform frontage. These detracted from the dignity of the stone buildings but added to their distinctiveness, and to passenger comfort! William Bell is believed to have designed these and similar stations built in the 1880s at Byers Green, Coundon, and Witton-le-Wear in County Durham. All stations handled goods traffic; substantial goods sheds were prominent features.

Ken Hoole (1984) classified Alnwick-Coldstream stations in ascending order of building size:

A Single-storey. Separate house: Edlingham, Kirknewton
B Island platform. Separate house: Whittingham
C Two-storey including house: Glanton, Hedgeley, Wooperton, Ilderton, Mindrum
D Ditto, but larger: Akeld
E Ditto, but larger still: Wooler.

Edlingham and Kirknewton

Edlingham served a sparsely populated area. It shared the smallest style of building with Kirknewton. Instead of the standard arrangement of waiting accommodation, a small timber and glass verandah was fitted between the building's twin pavilions. Edlingham was the least used branch station - 1,819 tickets issued in 1911 - whilst Kirknewton issued 3,213. Edlingham's booking office closed and the station was demoted to a halt in 1926. In common with most stations on the branch there were two tracks but only one platform, restricting the number of places where passenger trains could cross. Both stations are in residential use.

Whittingham

The NER built numerous island platform stations in the 1880s. Examples were at Elswick, and on the Newcastle-South Shields, Middlesbrough-Saltburn, and York-Church Fenton lines, also -for no obvious reason - at Whittingham! This is the only NER example on an otherwise single-track railway. The platform arrangement enabled passenger trains to cross, but at Wooler this was achieved with conventional, flanking platforms. Passenger facilities and offices on Whittingham's platform were within a long, rather plain single-storey building surrounded by a shallow glazed awning carried on fancy iron brackets, incorporating the Star of David - a motif also used at Elswick. Standing aloof were the stationmaster's house (a scaled-down version of main buildings at the other branch stations) and a row of cottages. After Wooler, this was the busiest station, booking 6,942 passengers in 1911. A variety of traffic was handled, including livestock (a mart adjoined the station), grain, coal and tiles. The platform and station building, complete with glassless awning, survive in a neglected state, accompanied by the former goods shed, coal office and decayed coal cells. The station house and cottages are still occupied.

Glanton, Hedgeley, Wooperton, Ilderton, and Mindrum

These single platform stations were alike, each with attractive, commodious buildings and the large wood-and-glass waiting areas. The stationmaster was housed in the double-storey section, whilst the booking office and public toilets were in the single-storey end block. A solid, imposing goods shed was provided. Each of these stations is well maintained and in residential use. For some years Ilderton was used as a restaurant, and it has timber and glass waiting rooms. In 1998 a short section of track had been re-laid and a passenger coach stood at the platform. At Mindrum a conservatory has replaced the waiting rooms.

Wooler

The principal intermediate station was on the edge of the town. In 1911, 13,199 tickets were issued, three times that recorded at most of the other branch stations. Two passenger platforms were connected by a footbridge. A fine range of buildings graced the down platform, including the familiar station house, with minor differences in the layout of the first floor windows and gables, and a lengthy single-storey block for public and office functions. The exterior was adorned with a shallow, slanting glazed awning on iron brackets - a smaller version was at other stations including Wooperton and Akeld. On the up platform was an enclosed waiting shed with a slanting roof, resembling the structures added to many of the station houses along the branch. The station building remains in residential/commercial use, and a goods shed survives, complete with awning.

Akeld

Another single platform station, the building here closely resembled that at Wooler but the single-storey office section and the entrance awning were much smaller. The station building is in residential use. The attached wood-and-glass shelter on the platform elevation has been reinstated in the style of the original structure. A brake-van stands at the goods platform.

By the standards of the Alnwick-Coldstream line, Kirknewton station had a modest building. Since closure it has been converted into a charming country residence.
(Martin Bairstow Collection)

The minor station at Mindrum was provided with splendid buildings, including the goods shed, seen in the background.
(Alan Young Collection)

Wooperton, looking north in 1950, twenty years after passenger services were withdrawn.
(Locomotive & General Railway Photographs)

Table 82 — CHATHILL and SEAHOUSES (North Sunderland Railway) — Summer 1950

WEEKDAYS

Miles		am	am	am	am	pm	pm
	3 Edinburgh ...... dep	....	....	6 55	10E40	2F30	..
	3 Berwick .. ,,	7 18	..	9 8	12E27	4 55	..
	3 Newcastle ...... dep	..	7 15	9 30	12p25	4G18	5 52
		am	am	am	pm	pm	pm
—	CHATHILL .. dep	8 10	9 40	10 50	1 50	5 50	7 20
—	North Sunderland ,,	8 27	9 57	11	1 7	7	7 37
4	SEAHOUSES .. arr	8 30	10 0	11 10	2 10	6 10	7 40

WEEKDAYS

Miles		am	am	am	pm	pm	pm
		am	am	am	pm	pm	pm
—	SEAHOUSES.... dep	7 35	9 15	10 10	12 50	4 40	6 45
	North Sunderland .. ,,	7 38	9 18	10 13	12 53	4 43	6 48
4	CHATHILL ..... arr	7 55	9 35	10 30	1 10	5 0	7 5
		am	am	am	pm	pm	pm
50	3 Newcastle .. arr	9 29	10K58	..	2D39	7N25	11A10
25	3 Berwick .. arr	....	....	11 15	2H12	6J29	7B51
82½	3 Edinburgh .. ,,	....	....	12p48	3 41	9 13	10 50

A—On Saturdays arrives Newcastle 10.48 am.
B—On Saturdays arrives Berwick 7.54 pm.
D—On Saturdays to 26th August inclusive arrives Newcastle 2.54 pm and commencing 2nd September 2.41 pm.
E—On Saturdays until 26th August inclusive departs Edinburgh 10.47 am and Berwick 12.55 pm.
F—On Saturdays departs Edinburgh 2.40 pm.
G—On Saturdays departs Newcastle 4.10 pm.
H On Saturdays, commencing 1st July arrives Berwick 1.57 pm.
J—On Saturdays arrives Berwick 6.36 pm.
K—On Saturdays arrives Newcastle 11.3 am.
N—On Saturdays arrives Newcastle 6.16 pm.
p—pm.

Table 67 — BERWICK-UPON-TWEED and KELSO — Summer 1955

WEEKDAYS

Miles		A am	A am	SX A pm	SO A pm	A pm		
	3 Newcastle.. dep	4 15	6 45	12J20	12C20	4B18	....	
	3 Edinburgh (Wav.) .. ,,	..	6 53	2 0	2K15	5 14	..	
—	BERWICK-upon-TWEED Z dep	6 30	9 20	3 28	3 40	6 47	..	
1½	Tweedmouth { arr	6 33	9 23	3 31	3 43	6 50	..	
	{ dep	6 40	9 28	3 36	3 48	6 55	..	
5¼	Velvet Hall ,,	6 47	9 35	3 43	3 55	7 2	..	
7½	Norham .. ,,	6 52	9 40	3 48	4 0	7 7	..	
10¾	Twizell .... ,,	6 57	9 45	3 53	4 5	7 12	..	
13½	Coldstream ...... ,,	7 9	9 54	4 3	4 15	7 20	..	
16½	Sunilaws ...... ,,	7 13	10 4	4 9	4 21	7 26	..	
19	Carham ...... ,,	7 18	..	4 14	4 26	..	..	
21½	Sprouston...... ,,	7 23	10 9	4 19	4 31	7 35	..	
23½	KELSO arr	7 28	10 14	4 24	4 36	7 40	..	
35	St. Boswells .. arr	8 7	10 56	4 56	5 8	8 15	..	

WEEKDAYS

Miles		A am	SO A am	SX A am	A pm	A pm		
	St. Boswells dep	6 22	8 33	8 33	4 5	7 15	....	
—	KELSO ...... dep	7 35	9 17	9 30	4 40	8 0	..	
2½	Sprouston .. ,,	..	9 22	9 35	4 45	8 5	..	
4¼	Carham .. ,,	..	9 27	9 40	4 50	..	..	
6¾	Sunilaws .. ,,	7 47	9 32	9 45	4 55	8 14	..	
10	Coldstream .. ,,	7 57	9 40	9 54	5 5	8 23	..	
12½	Twizell .. ,,	8 3	9 47	10 0	5 11	8 29	..	
15½	Norham .. ,,	8 9	9 53	10 6	5 17	8 35	..	
18½	Velvet Hall ,,	8 16	10 0	10 13	5 24	8 42	..	
22½	Tweedmouth { arr	8 23	10 7	10 20	5 31	8 49	..	
23½	{ dep	8 29	10 12	10 25	5 37	8 54	..	
	BERWICK-upon-TWEED Z arr	8 32	10 15	10 28	5 40	8 57	..	
81	3 Edinburgh arr	..	12D35	12 35	9 3	10 30	..	
90½	3 Newcastle ,,	10643	12 58	12L47	7E40	11H 8	..	

A—Through Trains between Berwick-upon-Tweed and St. Boswells.
B—Connection at Tweedmouth. On Sats. departs Newcastle 4.1 pm.
C—From 2nd July to 27th August inclusive departs Newcastle 1.18 pm.
D—From 9th July to 27th August inclusive arrives Edinburgh 11.38 am.
E—Arrives Newcastle 7.32 pm Fridays and 7.26 pm Saturdays.
G—Connection at Tweedmouth. On Saturdays arrives Newcastle 10.48 am.
H—On Saturdays arrives Newcastle 10.48 pm. Connection at Tweedmouth.
J—On Tuesdays and Thursdays 5th July to 25th Aug. departs Newcastle 12.35 pm.
K—On 18th June and on 10th and 17th September departs Edinburgh 2.0 pm.
L—On Mondays, 13th, 20th June and 12th September, also Fridays 24th June and 16th September arrives Newcastle 12.58 pm.
S or SO—Saturdays only.
SX—Saturdays excepted.
Z—For other trains between Berwick-upon-Tweed and Tweedmouth see Table 3.

The North Sunderland Railway

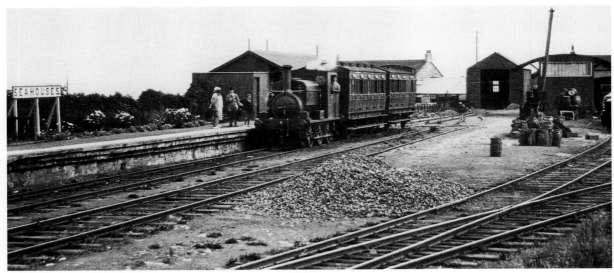

Manning Wardle 0-6-0 saddle tank Bamburgh with two ex-NER coaches at Seahouses in the 1920s.
(Peter E Baughan Collection)

Alan Wright's definitive work *The North Sunderland Railway* is recommended reading, from which much of the material in this chapter has been drawn.

This four-mile branch was among Britain's oddest railways. Its birth, operation, and even the nature of its passing were unusual. The East Coast main line avoided the coastal villages of Beadnell, Seahouses, and Bamburgh. Seahouses developed in the late 19th Century as a fishing port, but fishermen were disadvantaged by isolation from the railways. Fish was transported over roads of indifferent quality to Chathill station, four miles away. The North Eastern Railway showed no interest in serving Seahouses, so local people took the initiative. The Trustees of Lord Crewe were the major local landowners. They enlarged Seahouses harbour in 1886-88 (involving the temporary installation of a standard gauge railway), and led the campaign to link Seahouses to the national railway system. The fishing industry's interests were paramount, but the area was thought ripe for tourist development. The line's promoters considered creating a resort - St Aidan's-on-the-Sea - between Seahouses and Bamburgh. A Private Bill (1892) resulted in the North Sunderland Railway Act. (North Sunderland was the original village and parish, Seahouses a later extension.)

The route of the standard gauge, single-track railway was more-or-less direct from Chathill to Seahouses. In 1898 the NSR obtained permission to extend to Bamburgh, under the Light Railways Act (1896) and construct and operate the Chathill-Seahouses route as a Light Railway too. The Act enabled railway construction in regions with limited traffic potential, but where economic growth might be stimulated and communities could benefit from improved access. Light railways had less stringent regulations and signalling arrangements and could be constructed more cheaply. The North Sunderland Railway was possibly the first built under the Act. Fund-raising for construction was slow. Lord Armstrong, of Bamburgh Castle, contributed; he supported the Bamburgh extension. Savings were made by Light Railway designation, abandoning plans for Fleetham station, and by persuading the NER to allow the NSR to share Chathill station: the up platform would have a bay behind for Seahouses trains. Goods services began on 1 August 1898. Passenger services started on 18 December 1898, after improvements had been made to satisfy the Board of Trade.

The route crossed gently undulating countryside. After a 10-chain curve and run-round loop, immediately north of Chathill, the route deviated only slightly from a straight line, and gradients nowhere exceeded 1 in 80. Much of the journey was in shallow cuttings or on low embankments. Three streams were crossed, and there were bridges under two minor roads. There were level crossings over a farm track and two minor public roads. Before World War I, a quarry at Pasture Hill was served by a siding.

NSR passenger trains connected with NER trains. The NER agreed to maintain a 'local' stopping service to Chathill and arranged for certain express trains to call. The 1898 branch service was seven trains each way, taking 15 minutes on the journey. The branch engine was stabled at Seahouses, so the first train of the day was from Seahouses, and the final train terminated there. The number of trains hardly changed over the years, with about six each way per day, though in 1915 there were only four daily up workings. Timings were adjusted to keep in line with connecting ECML trains. Sunday trains, introduced in 1934, ceased in World War II. From 1939 the journey time increased to 20 minutes, when a 15mph speed limit was introduced because of the poor condition of the track.

Although never part of Lt-Col. Stephens' independent minor railways 'empire', the North Sunderland shared many of their features. It struggled to make a profit. Station buildings at North Sunderland and Seahouses were spartan, single-storey, corrugated iron affairs. The NSR could not afford to build a house for Seahouses' stationmaster. Signals were installed only at Chathill, and at Seahouses where there were ground signals. Ground frames sufficed for operating points at sidings.

The company's first locomotive, an 0-6-0 Manning Wardle Saddle Tank *Bamburgh*, was acquired on hire purchase. It gave almost half a century's service, expiring only four years before the line itself. The five original coaches were cast-off Highland Railway four-wheelers. Within their first week of NSR service they were sold to the Yorkshire Wagon & Finance Co. to raise cash to pay the contractor! These coaches were used until 1911-13,

LNER/BR Class Y7 0-4-0T No 68089 in the North Sunderland Railway shed at Seahouses on 1 August 1950. *(J C W Halliday)*

Bamburgh in the Seahouses bay platform at Chathill.
(LCGB Ken Nunn Collection)

Armstrong Whitworth diesel locomotive *The Lady Armstrong* at Seahouses.
(Peter Sunderland Collection)

to be replaced with 30 year-old ex-NER stock. In 1937, three ex-Great Eastern six-wheel coaches were acquired. Goods waggons were lent to the North Sunderland Railway by the NER / LNER. However the NSR created improvised stone trucks by decapitating two Highland Railway coaches. In the 1930s, economising wherever possible, the NSR neglected track maintenance, and experimented with diesel traction. An Armstrong-Whitworth diesel-electric shunter successfully operated passenger and mixed trains from 1933-34, so a similar locomotive was bought, to be named *The Lady Armstrong*. It ran until 1946. The NSR with only one, or, at best, two locomotives relied from time-to-time on help from NER, LNER, and BR engines. These included class H2 0-6-0 tanks, LNER J79, and finally Y7 0-4-0; when the latter was unavailable in autumn 1948, the NSR provided taxis for passengers. Lacking normal signals, the line operated the 'one engine in steam' principle. By attaching goods waggons to some passenger trains, movements were reduced. Sometimes, however, two locomotives worked simultaneously on the branch. Special working arrangements allowed a fish train to precede the afternoon train to Chathill. During World War II one engine operated the branch while another shunted at Seahouses yard.

Funds did not stretch to building the Bamburgh extension. (Access would have involved a reversal at Seahouses.) Instead, with NSR consent, a Mrs Cuthbertson operated a horse-drawn conveyance between Bamburgh and Seahouses to connect with trains. This facility continued until 1905, after which the operator offered a road motor service. Even before 1914, motor-car competition was apparent, but the NSR carried about 20,000 passengers a year in the mid-1920s. Goods traffic (chiefly coal and salt to Seahouses, and fish in the opposite direction) halved between 1910 and 1925.

The NSR depended heavily upon the NER, the LNER, and later BR(NER). The main line conveyed passengers to and from the branch, operated Chathill station, and issued tickets to North Sunderland and Seahouses. The NER/LNER and BR printed tickets issued at North Sunderland and Seahouses. Until 1936 excursion trains visited the branch, an NSR locomotive hauling main line coaches between Chathill and Seahouses. Waggons and locomotives were supplied, when required, by the main line operator. These favours came at a price. NSR's debts to the LNER mounted until 1939 when the LNER took control, although the NSR officially remained independent. After Nationalisation (1948) the NSR continued its ambiguous existence, independent in name, but reliant upon the British Transport Commission for motive power. Financial matters reached a head in July 1951 when the BTC advised the NSR that the 1939 LNER/NSR operating agreement was to be cancelled, and motive power withdrawn. NSR debts continued to mount. The condition of the track was such that only one obsolete class of BR(NER) locomotive could

safely use it. The coaches were life-expired. The BTC operated United Chathill-Seahouses buses, duplicating the railway service, and could carry the railway mail traffic. British Railways' road services could replace the NSR for parcels and goods, operating between Chathill or Belford, Seahouses, and other villages.

The final train, carrying some fifty passengers, left Seahouses at 4.20 pm on Saturday 27 October 1951, behind class Y7 locomotive no. 68089. It carried an unofficial headboard *Farne Islander*. The day's three later trains were cancelled, with taxis run instead. The official closure date for all traffic was 29 October 1951. Track lifting took place in 1953. Much of the trackbed is visible today.

Stations

North Sunderland probably opened with the line. NSR, *Bradshaw,* and derivative timetables omitted it for many years. As late as 1931 the NSR's own timetable handbill omitted North Sunderland. From 1934 *Bradshaw* included it in a timetable laid out in narrative, rather than columnar, form. Later columnar timetables gave no mileage for the station. The single platform and building were south east of the track. A siding was at the Chathill end, northwest of the track, entered from the Seahouses direction. The building, of corrugated iron with a lean-to awning, adjoined the level crossing, set back from the track and detached from the platform. A small extension was added after 1901 when the train guard took up residence, his wife acting as crossing keeper. In 1925 the timber platform was replaced with a brick structure, stone-edged, and backed by a brick wall. Goods services ceased in February 1928. A photograph of 1934 shows the short platform, a large nameboard with dark sans-serif lettering on a white ground, and lit by one oil lamp. Electric lighting was later installed. After closure the building was used by scouts, but it is no longer standing.

Seahouses station's single platform and building were northwest of the track. The pitched-roofed building was of corrugated iron. It contained (from the northeast) the stationmaster's and booking offices; waiting room and parcels office; ladies' waiting room and lavatory; and (in an 'extension') the gentlemen's lavatory. The stationmaster's/ booking office extended the full depth of the building, but the remaining sections were recessed, so the roof served as an awning. Oil lighting gave way to electricity in 1926. The trackwork included an extension of the passenger line into the engine shed, and southeast of the passenger platform were a run-round loop and two sidings. One served the fish loading area; the other was a public siding with coal pens, a crane, and a warehouse. The iron engine shed and warehouse had curved roofs, but in 1902 the engine shed received a slate pitched roof instead. After closure, the former stationmaster acted as BR and British Road Services agent in the station building, whilst BRS used the warehouse. By the early 1970s the site was a car park.

Berwick – Kelso – St Boswells

Coldstream, looking south in early LNER days. The station possessed elegant buildings as well as a stone
signal box (not seen in this view)
(Stations UK)

This 23½-mile route connected Tweedmouth with
the North British Railway's Waverley Line at St
Boswells. It closely followed the River Tweed
through the rich farmlands surrounding Kelso,
known as the Merse. At Coldstream it met the line to
Wooler and Alnwick, and at Roxburgh a branch left
for Jedburgh.

In 1811 (fourteen years before the Stockton-
Darlington line opened) an Act of Parliament
authorised a public Berwick-Kelso horse-drawn
railway, part of a scheme to link Berwick with
Glasgow. Insufficient funds were raised, and there
were legal complications because the line crossed a
detached part of County Durham in the Norham
area, finally absorbed by Northumberland in 1844.
The scheme was abandoned in 1827. Despite
renewed interest in 1836, again there was
insufficient financial support.

The Newcastle & Berwick Railway's Berwick-
Kelso route was approved by Parliament in 1845. It
opened from Tweedmouth to Sprouston,
Roxburghshire, 3½ miles into Scotland, in 1849. This
was the only instance of an English company's line
entering Scotland. In 1850 an eleven-mile North
British Railway line from St Boswells (then called
Newtown) to Wallace Nick, near Kelso, opened. This
joined the Tweedmouth-Sprouston route in 1851;
the two lines met end-on, not at Sprouston station,
but at Sprouston Junction, one mile southwest. A
new Kelso station replaced Wallace Nick.

Intermediate stations opened with the line, except
Sunilaws, opened (as Wark) in 1859 and Twizell,
opened in 1861. The Jedburgh branch opened in
1856, and Coldstream-Alnwick in 1887.

The route was originally double track. Though far
from straight, curves were gentle, and gradients
nowhere exceeded 1 in 140 on the NER stretch,
although the approach to Kelso from Sprouston
Junction reached 1 in 72. The country traversed was
undulating. No tunnels were needed, but much of
the route required embankments or cuttings. The
deepest cutting (30ft) was a little north of
Coldstream. The River Till was crossed at Twizell,
and the Teviot at Roxburgh. Several modest
masonry viaducts were required:

Grindon Burn (Newbiggin Dene):
      6 segmental arches, 134yd long,
      and 103ft high.
River Till: 6 segmental arches, 133yd long,
      89ft high.
East Learmouth: 5 semicircular arches, 94yd long,
      60ft high.
West Learmouth: 7 semicircular arches, 118yd long,
      62ft high.

The absorption of the Berwick & Kelso by the
NER was, in some measure, a response to the NBR's
ambitions to enter Northumberland. Reflecting their
strained relationship, Tweedmouth-St Boswells was
operated as two Kelso branches by the NBR and
NER. When the LNER absorbed both companies, the

'two branch' arrangement persisted as far as advertised services were concerned. The North Eastern Region passenger timetable of winter 1963 still showed only the Berwick-Kelso service; the Scottish volume generously included the entire Berwick-St Boswells line. The two Kelso 'branches' had a modest service of passenger trains. In 1863 there were four weekday return workings between Berwick and Kelso (two on Sunday) and seven weekday return services between Kelso and St Boswells. In 1910 there were five regular weekday trains each way between Berwick and Kelso, and six between Kelso and St Boswells. Each section had two Sunday trains. There was no apparent attempt to make services connect at Kelso. Berwick-Kelso trains made leisurely progress, taking an hour, stopping at all stations and reversing at Tweedmouth. Berwick-Kelso passenger trains ran beyond Tweedmouth up platform; the engine ran round to draw the coaches into the down platform and uplift passengers. Kelso-Berwick trains entered Tweedmouth down platform directly, and the engine ran round before proceeding to Berwick.

The NER worked passenger services with BTP A and O class tank locomotives stabled at Tweedmouth. C and P class 0-6-0 tender engines hauled goods services. Locomotive sheds were also at Kelso, Berwick (North British: closed by 1924), and Sprouston (closed 1916). Under LNER control locomotive workings on the Berwick-St Boswells

circle of routes via Kelso and Duns were integrated, using engines from four local sheds (Tweedmouth, Jedburgh, St Boswells, and Duns). Hoole notes, for instance, that in 1939 the St Boswells engine worked via Duns to Berwick, then Tweedmouth-Kelso-Berwick-Kelso-St Boswells. Sentinel railcars were used for some LNER workings. In about 1933 the LNER singled the track west of Kelso.

The 1943 timetable showed three weekday return passenger trains between Berwick and Kelso, with a further morning return working between Berwick and Coldstream. On the singled section, six weekday return trains (seven on Saturday) were provided. There were no Sunday trains. In August 1948 the main line north of Berwick was breached by floods. Edinburgh-London King's Cross services, such as *Flying Scotsman*, hauled by A4 Pacifics were diverted through Kelso. The south-facing junction at Tweedmouth enabled these expresses to run without reversal. Some services managed non-stop journeys between the capitals, despite the additional fifteen miles. The 1953 passenger timetable advertised four through return workings on weekdays between Berwick and St Boswells, with an extra return between St Boswells and Kelso. In 1955 lightly-used stations at Velvet Hall, Twizell (unstaffed since 1953), Sunilaws, Carham, and Sprouston closed to passengers. By winter 1962 only two weekday services worked from St Boswells (dep 8.25 am and 4.2 pm) to Berwick, with

A view from the 9.20 am Berwick-St Boswells train at Twizell on 26 April 1952. *(J W Armstrong Trust)*

return workings leaving Berwick at 9.56 am and 6.35 pm. A seven-minute turnaround was allowed at Tweedmouth. Two further St Boswells-Kelso return workings were shown. Whilst dmus operated most rural services, a steam locomotive and single coach were considered adequate for Berwick-Kelso.

Passenger traffic was supplemented by goods, principally cereals and potatoes outwards, and coal, lime, fodder, and livestock inwards. Norham also dispatched milk churns, cases of eggs, and boxes of wild rabbits in passenger trains. Away from stations, sidings were at West Ord (Tweedmouth/Velvet Hall); West Learmouth; and Shidlaw tileworks (Sunilaws/Carham).

The *Beeching Report* included Berwick-St Boswells among routes already earmarked for closure. Passenger services ended on 15 June 1964. The NER summer 1964 timetable failed to mention the closure: a sad end for an obscure line. Its value as a diversionary route probably enabled the line to survive as long as it did. Tweedmouth-Kelso goods services continued until 1965 (serving several former passenger stations). The down line was lifted in 1966 and the up line in 1969-70. Kelso-St Boswells goods services lasted until 1968.

Stations *(Tweedmouth-Kelso only)*

Velvet Hall took its name from a nearby house; the closest village, Horncliffe, was a mile away. Norham's villagers had over ½ mile to travel to their station. Twizell served countryside with scattered farms. It took its name (Old English for 'river confluence') from a ruined castle and bridge over the River Till. Situated close to the Tweed, but without a bridge across it, the station's catchment was limited to the English bank. For some years after it opened, Twizell was a request stop. The Berwickshire town of Coldstream's station was over a mile distant, in the Northumbrian hamlet of Cornhill. Before 1873 the station was called Cornhill - causing confusion with Cornhill in Banffshire. The next station was originally named Wark, after a village one mile away. In 1871 it was renamed Sunilaws after a nearby house, to distinguish it from Wark between Hexham and Reedsmouth. Carham was the first station into Scotland, but the hamlet was a mile away, and in Northumberland! Sprouston station was actually on the outskirts of its village. Kelso is north of the Tweed, but the station was almost a mile south of the river, at Maxwellheugh; the station and goods yard encouraged this settlement to develop into a suburb of Kelso.

Each station had two passenger platforms (plus a bay at Kelso). Benjamin Green designed the main buildings at the original stations east of Kelso. They were less elaborate than his main line stations, because, by 1849, the Newcastle & Berwick Railway was on an economy drive. Nevertheless, attractive structures were built at Velvet Hall, Coldstream, and Sprouston, with plainer buildings elsewhere. All main buildings were of stone. The platforms at stations (except Kelso) had fine casement oil-lamps.

Passenger traffic was light, as indicated below:

Tickets issued (English stations)

Station	1911	1951
Velvet Hall	9,582	176
Norham	14,277	701
Twizell	3,614	537
Coldstream	22,341	1,366
Sunilaws	3,268	no data

Velvet Hall had a sturdy two-storey house and offices on the down (Kelso-bound) platform, its plainness relieved by two cross-gable windows. In 1905 the structure was extended northeastwards. A goods shed adjoined immediately to the southwest. The up platform had a wooden, enclosed waiting shed with glazed front and diagonal boarding, of rabbit-hutch style, with an unusually high roof. The signal box, wooden on a stone base, was at the southwest end of the platform. The station building is in residential use, with offices in a modern extension.

Norham station was situated on an embankment, the upper of the two floors of the main building reaching the down platform. Mullion windows added some distinction. It was accompanied by a further wooden structure with discordant rooflines. The signal box was originally part of the down platform's suite of buildings, but, shortly after 1900, its replacement was constructed on the up platform. A sleeper crossing gave access to the up platform, with a shelter of the Velvet Hall style. After closure, the last stationmaster bought the property and converted the platforms into a railway museum. The wonderfully conserved site contains the signal box, coal depot, and the goods shed, which Wells (1998) suggests might originally have been an engine shed.

Twizell's down platform had an enclosed timber passenger shed and a further lock-up, both at the north end. Close by, a sleeper crossing accessed the signal box - a tall, hipped roof design of wood on a brick base - and a path to the up platform. This platform was displaced 50yd south of its neighbour. A group of mean, single-storey buildings adjoined the north ramp. An 1882 plan suggests that the up platform formerly extended to the sleeper crossing. The goods facilities were on the down side, immediately north of the passenger station. By 1976 the buildings had gone. Now only the overgrown platforms remain, with railway cottages nearby.

Coldstream's main passenger facilities were on the up platform, including a two-storey house with a bay window and corbelled-out gable and blind arch (reminiscent of Chathill) and an adjoining single-storey booking/parcels office. A separate block contained waiting rooms and the porters'/lamp room. On the down platform a suite of single-storey buildings included waiting rooms, an open-fronted shelter, and toilets. A standard NER footbridge was provided. Goods facilities were north of the up platform, whilst two sidings

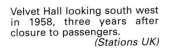
Velvet Hall looking south west in 1958, three years after closure to passengers.
(Stations UK)

Sunilaws in January 1976, looking towards Kelso.
(Alan Young)

Carham station was in Roxburghshire whilst the hamlet it served was in Northumberland. In this undated view, looking southwest, the staggered platform layout is clearly shown.
(Courtesy Ken Hoole Study Centre, Darlington)

and a water tower were behind the down platform. From 1887-1930 Coldstream was the junction and northern terminus for Alnwick (via Wooler) passenger services. By 1975 the site was occupied by a housing estate.

Sunilaws. The platforms were staggered either side of a level crossing. The main passenger facilities on the up platform, west of the crossing, included an attractive two-storey house/offices. The goods yard was opposite, on the down side. The other passenger platform had a wooden waiting shed and a pitched-roof brick and wood signal box. The station house (with NER clock) and platforms are well preserved.

Carham. Under BR administration, the NE and ScR boundary here coincided with the Anglo-Scottish border, so Carham was in the Scottish Region. It had staggered platforms either side of a level crossing, the up platform to the east. The house on this platform resembled that at Sunilaws. The down platform had a lock-up and an enclosed timber shelter. A signal box (Sunilaws style) stood opposite the down platform. By 1976 only the platforms remained.

Sprouston, several miles into Scotland, was the final N&B station. On the up platform the station house and booking facilities were in a two-storey building, distinguished by prominent gables with eaves (rather than raised gables) on the platform elevation. An engine shed and water tower stood north of the platform. The original shed was wooden; it blew down in 1881, and its brick replacement survived until the mid-1960s. A further residence and brick waiting shelter stood on the down platform, with a signal box beyond its north ramp. This box was installed in 1912, replacing one diagonally across the level crossing. The station house is in residential use, its garden occupying the trackbed.

Kelso station's up platform had a bay at the Berwick end, where there was also a goods depot. The smart, two-storey main building had a gable and two dormers facing the through platform and two further dormers facing the bay. Part of the building was recessed to accommodate enclosed waiting facilities, and there was a large awning. The down platform possessed a signal box, water tower, water crane, and shelter, with a siding to its rear. The metal footbridge featured diagonal latticework sides. Unlike its neighbours Kelso was gas-lit, and it received Scottish Region totem name signs. By 1976 the station was demolished.

Sprouston (Roxburghshire) in January 1976, looking towards Kelso. A typical NER footbridge formerly spanned the tracks. Today the station house is in residential use, and the trackbed is its garden.
(Alan Young)

An excellent general view of Norham, looking southwest. The station survives as a museum.
(Ken Hoole, courtesy Ken Hoole Study Centre, Darlington)

The Blyth & Tyne System

G5 0-4-4T No 67323 stands beneath the water-crane at Blyth. It is fitted for push-pull operation.
(E E Smith / N E Stead Collection)

With the exceptions of the East Coast main line and North Shields branch, the Blyth & Tyne Railway operated all passenger services in the southeast Northumberland coalfield. The B&T was independent until absorbed by the NER on 7 August 1874. Because the B&T line that became part of the 'Coast Circle' is described in *Suburban Railways of Tyneside*, references to the B&T from 1864 apply only to lines north of Backworth and Monkseaton.

Development of the B&T

The system's development is inseparable from the growth of mining. From the 16th Century coal was mined in shallow pits close to the Tyne. By the early 17th Century, there were pits further north. In 1605 Huntingdon Beaumont, a Nottinghamshire businessman, obtained permission to extract coal in Bedlingtonshire (then a detached part of County Durham). Beaumont had installed a wooden waggonway - possibly the world's first - at Wollaton (Notts.) to carry coal to the River Trent. He applied this technology to his Northumbrian operations, and by 1608 waggonways conveyed coal from his pits at Bedlington, Bebside, and Cowpen to the River Blyth. It was shipped to London, where coal from the 'Great Northern Coalfield' was in demand. Beaumont's pits proved unprofitable, and his

financial embarrassment caused the closure of his waggonways in 1618. It is probable that about a century passed before other waggonways opened in southeast Northumberland. Warn in *Waggonways and Early Railways of Northumberland* (1976) notes that the following routes operated in the 'Blyth & Tyne' area:

Plessey Waggonway - 4 miles to Blyth, open by 1699, closed 1812.
Black Close Colliery (near North Seaton) to the River Wansbeck, opened 1755.
Hartley to Seaton Sluice, opened by 1758.
Barrington to Bedlington Staith, opened by 1787
Cowpen to Blyth - 1¼ miles. Open by 1794; later incorporated into the B&T Railway.
Killingworth Waggonway - Killingworth / West Moor to Willington opened 1806-08, closed 1942.
West Moor to Burradon - opened 1820.
Netherton Waggonway - opened to Stobhill 1828 then to the Wansbeck 1829. Realigned to join the East Coast main line 1847.
Bedlington Ironworks to Barrington - opened 1821: the first line in the world to use malleable iron rails.
Cramlington Waggonway to Backworth and later Shankhouse and East Hartford. Opened 1823, closed 1898.

Netherton to Barrington and Bedlington - opened 1832.

West Cramlington to Backworth - opened 1838.

Most significant in B&T history was the Seghill Coal Company's waggonway. This firm used the Cramlington Waggonway but grew dissatisfied with the facility. Seghill's own line to the River Tyne at Percy Main opened for coal traffic on 1 June 1840. From 28 August 1841 passengers were conveyed in rope-hauled trains. Stations were at Seghill, Holywell, Prospect Hill, and Percy Main. From 1844 trains were locomotive-hauled; the carriages were low-roofed, spring-less, and uncomfortable. The Seghill railway was extended on 3 March 1847 when passenger trains reached Blyth, serving Seaton Delaval and Hartley Pit. This line was primarily to carry coal from pits near Blyth to the Tyne for export, since the River Blyth was shallow. By December 1847, what had become the Blyth, Seghill & Percy Main Railway was calling itself the Blyth & Tyne. The May 1849 timetable showed three weekday departures from Blyth for the hour-long journey to Percy Main, three return workings, and an extra Percy Main-Seaton Delaval train. From 1847-52 passengers could change at Hartley Pit onto a train that intermittently operated on a waggonway to Seaton Sluice via Dairy House. The service ceased when the B&T restricted passenger trains to their 'main' line. Seaton Sluice never again had passenger trains. Although the Collywell Bay branch reached the village from Monkseaton in 1914, it was not opened and was dismantled in 1931. (See *Suburban Railways of Tyneside*.)

From Newsham, the Bedlington Coal Company opened a 2¾-mile branch to Bedlington for coal traffic on 12 June 1850. The B&T provided passenger trains, from August 1850. In 1851 the service was three trains each way on weekdays, and two on Sunday - the same frequency as on the Blyth-Percy Main route. Passenger stations were at Newsham, Cowpen Lane (renamed Bebside in April 1860), and Bedlington. The B&T bought the line in 1855. A wooden viaduct 257yd long and about 80ft high crossed the River Blyth. In 1929 it was replaced with a steel structure, on a slight deviation.

Incorporated on 1 January 1853, the B&T braced itself to repel companies that might intrude on its patch. In August 1853 Royal Assent was obtained for their Newsham-Bedlington line - the B&T already operated passenger trains on this route for the Bedlington Coal Company - and on to Morpeth. This Assent also allowed upgrading of the Hartley-Dairy House waggonway. In July 1854 Parliament approved B&T plans to extend the latter route to Tynemouth and construct northwards to Longhirst on the East Coast main line. Passenger and goods trains were introduced between Bedlington and

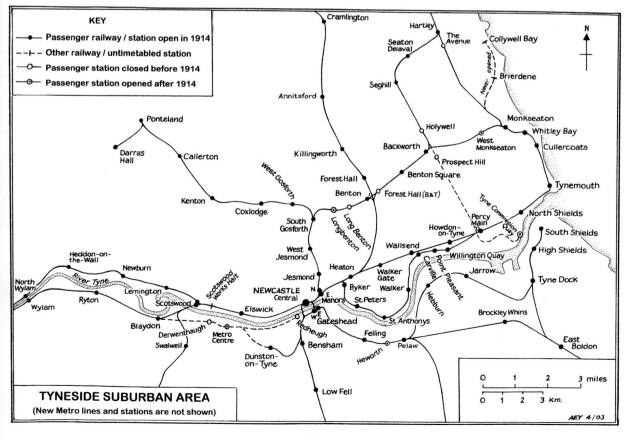

KEY

- ● Passenger railway / station open in 1914
- – ┼ – Other railway / untimetabled station
- ○ Passenger station closed before 1914
- ◉ Passenger station opened after 1914

TYNESIDE SUBURBAN AREA

(New Metro lines and stations are not shown)

AEY 4/03

The restrained but dignified exterior of Blyth, shortly before World War I
(Peter E Baughan Collection)

Morpeth on 1 April 1858. The track was single from Choppington to Morpeth (except through Hepscott). Until May 1880 Bedlington trains used Morpeth (B&T) station. The B&T reconsidered plans for northward extension, and in August 1857 Royal Assent was obtained for a Bedlington-Warkworth Harbour line via Bothal Demesne, Woodhorn, Linton, and Warkworth; the Longhirst scheme was dropped. The outcome was a two-mile branch to North Seaton that opened to all traffic on 7 November 1859. No further progress was made at this stage, but Assent was obtained in June 1861 for a branch to Newbiggin, upon which they did not act. In August 1867 a further Bill to construct to Warkworth Harbour, with a branch to Newbiggin, was successful. On 1 March 1872 the line beyond North Seaton opened, incorporating the first mile of the Warkworth Harbour line, and the 2¼-mile Newbiggin branch, which swung sharply east from the intended 'main line'. A massive wooden viaduct, 400yd in length and 85ft above water level crossed the River Wansbeck; it was reputedly the largest wooden structure in Britain. A steel structure replaced it in 1929. An intermediate station appeared in the timetable from May 1878 at Hirst, later renamed Ashington. The Warkworth Harbour line was never built, so Newbiggin remained the northerly passenger terminus. However a network of mineral lines eventually extended north to Ashington, Linton, Ellington, Lynemouth, Newbiggin, and Woodhorn collieries, and opencast mines at Longhirst (and more recently, Butterwell). The Alcan aluminium smelter, built in 1968, was also served. An addition to the ex-B&T system was mooted in 1894, when the NER sought to build a Blyth-Cramlington line. Opposition by Lord Hastings, who feared losing revenue from 'wayleaves' on existing routes through his land, caused the Bill's abandonment.

B&T motive power and freight traffic

Locomotives on the B&T before absorption by the NER were generally 2-4-0 tenders for passenger and goods, and 0-6-0 for coal trains. Various builders were used, including Robert Stephenson and Timothy Hackworth. Some engines were constructed by the B&T at Percy Main. In NER days, from 1874, freight was hauled by classes 8, 44, 59, 124, 290, and 398. From 1886 C class 0-6-0 and P class joined the others. On the coal staiths, shunting duties were left to 0-6-0 tanks, and later diesel classes 03 and 08. K1 and 4MT 2-6-0 locomotives hauled freight after Nationalisation, followed by diesel classes 17, 20, 37, and more recently class 56.

Shortly before World War I, G5 0-4-4Ts, operating push-and-pull 'autocars', took over many passenger duties. Passenger stock in NER/LNER days comprised a mixture of clerestory coaches (built 1896-1906), low-roofed stock (built 1899-1906) and later elliptical roofed coaches, all of NER origin. From 1927 the LNER introduced single-unit Sentinel Cammell and Clayton steam railcars in NE England. They operated on the former B&T lines; the Sentinel *Phenomena* spent its working life plying mainly between Blyth, Morpeth, and Monkseaton. From 1937 G5 push-and-pull operations were re-introduced, and steam railcars were abandoned by 1948. Passenger services to Blyth/Newbiggin were dieselised in September 1958. However the 5.30 am parcels train ex-Newcastle, returning as the 7.35 am ex-Newbiggin remained steam-hauled. Locomotives were stabled at Percy Main (formerly the company's workshop) until 1966; South Blyth (1879-1968); and North Blyth (1897-1968). Cambois diesel depot opened in 1968.

Although passenger services operated successfully for many years, goods and mineral traffic created the B&T and has sustained much of the system since 1964, when passenger trains ceased. Coal export via staiths at Blyth and (from 1867) Cambois was vital to the railway. To convey

G5 0-4-4T No 67323 at Newsham's up platform.

J21 0-6-0 No 65110 rolls into Choppington, on its way to Morpeth with an excursion.

coal to the ports, the network steadily improved in the late 19th Century. Pits west of Ashington were linked directly to the ex-B&T at Ashington in 1886, saving coal trains the circuitous journey via Pegswood, Morpeth (reverse), and Newsham (reverse again) to Blyth. The congested Newsham-Blyth staiths branch was supplemented by another line in 1888, the year when further staiths were built at Blyth. In the 1890s rail facilities at Cambois were enlarged, and staiths built at North Blyth. In 1896 a curve from Marchey's House Junction to Winning Junction opened off the Bedlington-Ashington line enabling Ashington coal to reach North Blyth / Cambois directly.

In the early 20th Century some fifty collieries operated in the ex-B&T area. Port facilities continued expanding, further staiths opening at Blyth in 1928. Blyth handled other freight too, including timber and fish. The port reached its zenith in the early-1960s when almost 6.9 million tonnes of coal were exported, making Blyth Europe's leading coal shipping port. However, from the mid-1960s Northumberland's collieries closed, leaving only Ellington in operation. The decline was partly offset by the opening of opencast mines, notably Butterwell (near Ashington) which prospered in the 1990s. Until its closure in 2001 the coal-fired power station at Cambois was served by rail, and the aluminium smelter at Lynemouth (opened 1968) still has double-track rail access. Throughout the 1950s road lorries lured freight away from Britain's railways. The ex-B&T system was no exception, with goods handling ceasing at all stations in 1963-65. Bedlington handled parcels traffic until 1966. By 1990 only coal, alumina, and aluminium were carried. West Blyth staiths closed in 1989, and a new facility opened at Bates in 1991. From 1980 a new curve between Hepscott North and Morpeth North junctions allowed direct access to and from Scotland. Former double-track sections were singled: Bedlington-Choppington (1973) and Newsham-Backworth (1985). Since 1980 a new single-track has allowed independent working from Backworth to Benton Quarry on the ECML, avoiding conflict with Metro services.

B&T passenger services

The B&T system's layout allowed many permutations of passenger services, and these changed over the years. *Bradshaw* of April 1910 showed an exceedingly complex set of train workings. By 1920 frequencies were generally reduced, except on the Manors North-Morpeth service. An intensive bus network developed in the 1920s between the closely spaced towns, and train loadings declined. Bedlington-Morpeth trains were particularly vulnerable to competition because the towns' stations were away from their centres. By summer 1946 only two trains used the route, both towards Morpeth. In summer 1948 only the 6.45 am ex-Blyth was running. A British Railways' review of the Bedlington-Morpeth service noted that 1,554

local and 76 other passengers were carried in 1948, receipts totalling £61. Parcels traffic was worth £198, but freight originating from the line earned £80,695! The review recognised that 'regular passenger traffic is negligible; the two branch stations are principally used on the annual Northumberland Miners' Gala day at Morpeth and for occasional excursions'. BR proposed closure to passengers, with occasional reopenings for Gala and excursion trains. Loss of passenger revenue was negligible, and income could be derived from letting the general and ladies' rooms at Choppington and Hepscott. Bedlington U.D.C.'s suggestion that reduced fares would attract custom found no favour with BR who withdrew the passenger train 1950. In the final months the two regular passengers were generously provided with three or four suburban coaches. How things had changed from 1911 when Choppington issued almost 116, 000 tickets!

By summer 1950 the B&T timetable was threadbare between weekday morning and evening peak hours; Monkseaton-Blyth had no service between the 9.12 am ex-Monkseaton and 4.40 pm ex-Blyth. Saturday trains were more numerous, as in previous years, catering for shopping and leisure journeys. From January 1955 the services were focussed on Monkseaton, to reduce operating costs and improve connections to north Tyneside suburban coastal stations. (Dmus were introduced in June 1958.) The revised weekday and Saturday services differed enough to require separate listings in the NE Region timetable. Sunday trains ceased by summer 1954.

Beeching earmarked the ex-B&T for closure, the proposal being published on 8 November 1963. On 30 July 1964, despite objections, the Minister of Transport consented to the withdrawal of passenger services. Blyth and Ashington, each with a population of about 30,000, would become two of the largest British towns to lose their trains, but the 'closure culture' was enormously strong - not least among BR senior officials. There was no inclination to improve and promote the service, practise economies such as de-staffing stations, or consider park-and-ride schemes. The final train left Blyth at 11.59 pm for Newbiggin on Saturday 31 October, and official closure took place on the following Monday. Freight services continued except for Monkseaton-Hartley, Woodhorn-Newbiggin, and Blyth Signal Box-Blyth station, which closed entirely. Some excursions continued from Newsham. In 1968 the Isabella-Blyth Shed branch closed. Since passenger closure ECML passenger trains have occasionally been diverted over the system - the Morpeth NE curve made this operation much simpler. However withdrawal of ECML overnight passenger services (1988), route electrification (1991), and bi-directional ECML signalling have reduced diversions. Forty years after their withdrawal, passenger services on the Backworth-Ashington section might be reinstated as a response to increased road congestion.

Seghill on 29 October 1960. Only a single platform was provided. Trains for Newbiggin had to cross onto the up line.

(Geoffrey C Lewthwaite)

In December 1972, eight years after closure, Seaton Delaval station was largely intact. In the background the huge pit heap of Seghill Colliery (closed in 1962) dominates the landscape. Today the station has gone, whilst the pit heap has been lowered and landscaped. *(Alan Young)*

Hartley in May 1959, seen from an Avenue Branch train. The curving platforms on the right were used by trains to and from Backworth.

(Ken Hoole, courtesy Ken Hoole Study Centre, Darlington)

Stations

Because stations opened at different times, and some were relocated or rebuilt, they varied in design. They were generally of limited architectural quality. Compared with most Northumbrian stations they were well patronised, as seen below. However comparison of 1911 and 1951 ticket issues shows the impact of bus competition. In 1951 Seghill, North Seaton, Ashington and Newbiggin had only 14% of the 1911 traffic; only Hartley (96%) significantly retained traffic.

	Tickets issued		Regular Passengers (TUCC Report 1964)
	1911	**1951**	
Seghill	39,020	5,499	23
Seaton Delaval	77,375	17,376	0
Hartley	46,999	45,135	100
Newsham	133,659	61,499	174
Blyth	348,623	62,594	74
Bebside	57,324	9,109	22
Bedlington	227,121	52,791	100-120
North Seaton	100,192	13,845	3
Ashington	257,883	39,778	54
Newbiggin	165,927	23,514	182
Choppington	115,642	closed	closed
Hepscott	13,961	closed	closed

Latterly all stations were gas lit, except Hepscott, with oil lanterns, and Choppington and Ashington with LNER electric lighting on swan-neck posts. LNER wooden nameboards with raised metal letters were standard; BR totem signs were not installed.

Holywell was an original Percy Main-Seghill station. In 1860 it was renamed Backworth. It closed in 1864 when Backworth (Hotspur) opened on the Newcastle-Gosforth-Coast line. For goods purposes Holywell retained its name until complete closure in 1965. In the 1960s a shortened platform and small wooden sheds survived.

Seghill also opened in 1841. Its layout was unconventional with only one platform, on the up line. Down trains reached the platform via crossover points. Passenger facilities were in a single-storey brick structure with a pitched roof and a central gabled vestibule set forward onto the platform. Originally it was embellished with kneelers (projections at the foot of the gable) and a ball finial on the vestibule gable. The building was probably constructed in the 1860s. Close to the level crossing the platform ended without a ramp, abutting the signal box. Latterly this was a small wooden structure, replacing one demolished in the 1940s by a land-mine. After closure in 1964 the building, platform and signal box remained intact in 1972. Ten years later these had all gone.

Seaton Delaval was called Seaton Delaval Colliery until 1864. The down platform possessed a plain, partially rendered station house, and a separate waiting room block. Both were of brick construction with pitched roofs. A small wooden shelter stood on the up platform. On the overbridge a timber shed, constructed in 1885, contained the booking office. The overbridge subsided in 1940, weighed down by a wartime barricade; for many years, girders supported it, obstructing the up line, so all trains used the down platform. By 1972 the elevated timber shed had gone, the road bridge was rebuilt, and two-track working was restored; the platforms and other buildings remained in place. The line is now single, and the station has gone.

Hartley Pit station adjoined Hester Pit. From 1847-52 passengers could change here for trains on a mineral line to Seaton Sluice. It was replaced by a new facility about 150yd northeast where the Avenue Branch to Whitley (Monkseaton) joined the Backworth line.

Hartley had two sharply curved platforms on the Seghill line and one (adjacent to double track) serving the Avenue Branch. A two-storey brick house stood between the diverging platforms presenting gable ends to each, with a single-storey block at the southern end. Segmental arched windows were provided. An additional brick building - still in residential use- and wooden shed also stood on the Avenue platform. About five years before closure a new signal box was installed where the Avenue and up-Seghill platforms converged. By 1972 the platforms were demolished.

The Avenue was possibly served by Hartley Pit-Seaton Sluice trains. Its official life began in 1861 with the inauguration of the Hartley-Whitley line. In *Bradshaw* of February 1863 the Avenue, with the footnote 'for Seaton Sluice and Delaval Hall', was served by all trains - four each way on weekdays and two on Sunday. The station closed with the line in 1864, never to reopen. It has been demolished.

Newsham opened at the junction of the Percy Main-Blyth with the Bedlington line, when the latter opened to passengers in 1850. Two platforms, connected by a subway, served the Bedlington line. The up platform's east face was for Blyth. The absence of a facing crossover at the Blyth end meant that Blyth to Newsham trains reached this platform by 'overshooting' and setting back. Newsham's buildings were austere. Three single-storey brick structures occupied the up/branch platform; one, rendered and run-down by the 1960s was the oldest surviving B&T station building. A further brick building, including a waiting room, was on the down platform. LNER nameboards reading 'Newsham change for Blyth' remained until closure, and some gas lamps carried rectangular orange name signs - either unusual BR additions, or over-painted LNER signs. By 1973 demolition was almost complete.

Blyth's first station opened in 1847 adjacent to the river. Wells (1989) notes that the wooden box-like structure was in Croft (later King) Street. In 1867 a larger station, to the west, replaced the original one. The new station was rebuilt in 1894-96. Its

Bebside, on 21 August 1964. Only ten weeks before closure, the smart, compact building on the up platform was well maintained.
(Ken Hoole, courtesy Ken Hoole Study Centre, Darlington)

Bedlington, seen from a passing train on 28 August 1963. As at Seghill, a single up line platform catered for through traffic in both directions.
(Ken Hoole, courtesy Ken Hoole Study Centre, Darlington)

Hepscott in April 1977, 27 years after closure to passengers, and before the NER signal box and traditional gates were taken out of use. The small sign (in orange and white) declaring the station to be closed and recommending alternative rail facilities, was a common fixture at North Eastern Region stations.
(Alan Young)

A rare view of North Seaton station in about 1910. The main building on the down platform closely resembled structures elsewhere on the B&T system at Ashington and Benton.
(Alan Young Collection)

Ashington, looking north, shortly before World War I. The Newbiggin line curves away sharply to the right, whilst the lines to the left serve the Ashington collieries.
(Alan Young Collection)

Ashington in 1958, looking south. The awning was an LNER addition. *(Stations UK)*

offices and passenger facilities were in a block transverse to the track. This was an architecturally restrained single-storey building in brick. The road frontage had a raised central section for the entrance surmounted by a gable (with clock), and a slanted glass awning. The single island platform was partly covered by a ridged awning with glazed roof and end-screens - closely resembling Felling (1896). Numerous sidings flanked the running lines. The station was demolished in 1972.

Bebside was called Cowpen Lane until 1860. Brick buildings stood on both platforms. The booking office and toilets on the up platform were in a structure of the Seghill type. The Seghill vestibule section was used for a square bay window at Bebside. On the other platform the buildings included an enclosed wooden waiting shed. In 1972, although the buildings had gone, the platforms were intact, but these have since been demolished.

Bedlington, like Seghill, had one platform, on the up side, used by trains in both directions. There was a bay for Newbiggin branch trains in the early days, when Bedlington-Morpeth was the 'main line'. The single-storey brick building presented an L-shape to the platform; its northern unit was of the Seghill type. A hipped glass awning was fitted within the L-plan, front-supported by iron pillars and small spandrels with quatrefoil motifs. In 1973 the track arrangement was changed to eliminate two-directional operation of the platform line, and the NER footbridge was dismantled. The platform

survives with two separate sections of the former buildings, the central portion having been demolished. Within sight of each other, Bedlington North and South signal boxes remain in use.

North Seaton's main building, on the up platform, resembled that at Benton (B&T). The two-storey station house had a raised gable on the platform elevation, with a slightly projecting ground floor bay window topped by a parapet. Slightly recessed, two single-storey blocks with roofs of differing heights adjoined the main house, and a small brick shed completed the ensemble. The station was demolished by 1972.

Ashington's main facilities were on the up platform. The principal building resembled North Seaton's, and had sundry additions including a waiting shelter. An austere two-storey house accompanied it. On the down platform, the substantial, plain, single-storey building had a timber-and-glass frontage. Additions to the buildings were made between 1895 and 1924. The up platform received a glazed, ridged awning, with wooden gables. The north end had a typical NER screen. In 1972 only the platforms remained.

Newbiggin was a mining village and aspiring coastal resort when the railway arrived in 1872. The station building was H-plan with an elongated central section. Dutch gables with finials adorned the two-storey west and single-storey east wings, making this the most attractive Blyth/Newbiggin area station. The platform elevation included a

A Metro Cammell dmu stands at the Newbiggin terminus.   *(Paul Aston / N E Stead Collection)*

49

On 10 June 1967 a SLS/MLS railtour borrowed the National Coal Board locomotive 0-6-0ST No 39 (built 1954), a brake van and coaches to visit the Ashington collieries. *(Martin Bairstow Collection)*

slightly projecting ground floor window on the west wing, and a Venetian window on the east wing. These window styles were repeated, with minor variations, on the road frontage. A verandah - removed before closure - stretched between the wings. The main platform (about 200yd) and bay (about 120yd) were extended by 43yd in 1902 to accommodate longer excursion trains. In 1924 the LNER planned additional capacity. Scheme 1 would double the line to Woodhorn (one mile west of Newbiggin) and create a new station with two curving 130yd platforms on sidings northwest of the original station. The main building, reached by a new approach road, would be on the up platform, with a waiting shed on the other platform. Scheme 2 was to add a 200yd platform opposite, but displaced westwards from, the existing main platform. Neither scheme was adopted. After closure the tracks were removed between Newbiggin and Woodhorn, and the station site was cleared by the mid-1970s.

Choppington was a busy station for many years, but ended its life in 1950, with only one daily weekday train. A few years earlier the LNER installed electric lighting and small name tablets. The station house of uncoursed stone and at right-angles to the down platform, adjoined the level crossing. By the early 1970s the buildings and platforms had been demolished.

Hepscott was a rural backwater, as 1911 bookings

testify. This was a two-platform station with the main building, a modest stone structure, on the down side. A crossing cottage, also in stone, accompanied it. An NER wooden shed on the up (north) platform took over the passenger functions of the original building, and the down platform was disused by 1914. After closure to passengers the up platform and two wooden buildings remained until at least 1963. Fourteen years later the old house and cottage were still occupied, accompanied by the NER signal box, and old crossing gates. The box closed in 1984 when automatic half-barriers were installed.

Morpeth (B&T) opened eleven years after the N&B station, and was immediately southeast. The substantial building was in random-coursed stone, with round-headed windows on the ground floor, and rectangular upstairs. Wansbeck Valley trains also used the station until 1872. After absorption into the NER, the station remained in use until 1880, when a short line was constructed to create a bay at the east end of the main line station's up platform. The B&T goods shed and station building are extant, the latter unoccupied in summer 2001.

Ashington Colliery, Ellington, Linton, and **North Moor** halts were on the 20-mile National Coal Board system, which operated until 1964. Equipped with short platforms, the halts served miners. Tank engines hauled the antiquated passenger stock.

The Newcastle and Carlisle Railway

V1 2-6-2T No 67658 at Hexham with a terminating local passenger train from Newcastle.

(N E Stead Collection)

The journey from Newcastle to Carlisle begins by crossing the Tyne (usually over King Edward Bridge) and follows the 'Durham bank' past the MetroCentre shopping mall, to Blaydon. From here the broad Tyne valley is largely rural, flanked by green hills and dotted with farmhouses and woodland. At intervals the railway closely follows the gradually narrowing river. The line re-enters Northumberland at Wylam. Reminders of the industrial age pass by the train window: the occasional spoil-heap colonised by trees, former sidings, and track-beds of railways that offered journeys to Allendale, Riccarton, Alston, and Brampton. After Haltwhistle the scenery becomes hillier as the line of Hadrian's Wall is crossed and Cumberland (now Cumbria) is entered, just beyond Gilsland. The remainder of the journey through undulating pastoral country is punctuated by Cowran Hills cutting and viaducts across deep gorges. There is not only fine scenery, but also an opportunity to admire historic railway architecture. 'Perhaps because it is now a secondary route, albeit an important one, it has retained more of its character than any other sixty miles of railway' (Biddle & Nock 1983). Several structures enjoy Grade II Listed status: Corby and Middle Gelt viaducts; Haltwhistle station building, signal box, water tank and water crane; and Stocksfield, Riding Mill and Corbridge stations. Wylam station is listed Grade II*.

This was the first railway to cross England between navigable waters of the west and east

coasts. It received the Royal Assent on 22 May 1829 and opened in stages between 1834 and 1838. Before the railway opened, the journey by horse-and-cart between Newcastle and Carlisle along the congested Military Road took two to three days. From the 1770s, there were plans for Tyne-Solway canals; Thomas Telford surveyed such a route in 1796. The terrain was difficult for canal construction, but such projects as the Rochdale Canal in the south Pennines demonstrated that canals could cross even more challenging landscapes. The decision to link the coasts by rail was influenced by the tradition of carrying coal by waggonways in Northumberland and Durham, and conveyance of coal from inland pits without access to navigable water was a major reason for the project.

The Newcastle-on-Tyne & Carlisle Railroad Company's plans faced opposition from over thirty landowners. The logical path followed the Tyne to Haltwhistle, then the Tipalt Burn valley. Beyond a low watershed, the River Irthing valley offered an easy route through Brampton and Hayton to Carlisle. Brampton's inhabitants feared that their town would face ruin if penetrated by the railway. Consequently the line passed 11/2 miles south - a cause of inconvenience in later years. Hayton was avoided at the insistence of Sir Hew Dalrymple Ross, who demanded substantial compensation for invasion of his privacy. The railway was therefore denied the Irthing valley route and forced southward into hillier country, where construction was difficult and expensive. Despite heavy earthworks the railway's path was awkward, with short straight sections and intervening tight curves. A continuous uphill gradient of 1 in 107 confronted trains for some four miles east of Wetheral. Viaducts were needed at Wetheral (188yd long, 5 arches, and 95ft high) and Corby (160yd long, 7 arches, and 70ft high). Between Brampton Junction and How Mill a 73ft high embankment and 40ft deep cutting were required at Hell Beck, and the world's largest cutting at that time was excavated through the Cowran Hills. Here, a tunnel was planned, but the sandy strata required a spectacular mile-long cutting, up to 110ft deep, widening to 305ft between the highest points, and supported by 14ft retaining walls.

Impressive engineering works were not limited to the Cumbrian section. At Wylam the railway was carried alongside the Tyne for ³/₄ mile on a wall 26ft above low water. At Warden, the South Tyne was crossed on a bridge with three stone piers, and wooden spans and platforms. (The wooden parts were replaced with cast iron in 1848.) The NER replaced this bridge in 1906 with a steel girder structure on realigned track. Two further bridges over the South Tyne, and one over the River Allen, were between Haydon Bridge and Bardon Mill. There were tunnels at Farnley, east of Corbridge (170yd), and Whitchester, east of Haltwhistle (202yd).

After route adjustments, some in response to criticisms by George Stephenson who examined the plans, 16³/₄ miles were completed between Blaydon and Hexham. Horse-drawn goods trains commenced in late-1834, and passenger services on 10 March 1835. Newcastle passengers reached Blaydon by coach or boat. Steam locomotives hauled passenger trains from the opening day when *Samson* and *Hercules* were on duty, the former built by Robert Stephenson & Company, the latter by R&W Hawthorn. The Act of 1829 permitted only horse traction, but in the intervening six years the Liverpool & Manchester and Stockton & Darlington had shown steam power's superiority. The N&C took the risk of using steam in contravention of the Act. However, Captain Charles Bacon Gray of Styford (Riding Mill), who had been obstructive to the N&CR from the outset, obtained an injunction to hold the N&CR to the terms of the Act. Rather than use horses, the company cancelled all trains from 28 March 1835. Aided by the public outcry that followed, the N&CR gained Bacon Gray and other landowners' agreement to the use of steam locomotives. Services resumed on 6 May, and an Act of 17 June permitted steam traction

On 11 June 1835 a 1¼-mile extension opened eastwards to Derwenthaugh, followed by 7½ miles from Hexham to Haydon Bridge on 28 June. Blenkinsopp Colliery, near Haltwhistle, to Carlisle (20 miles), opened on 19 July 1836. On 1 March 1837 trains were introduced on the 2½ miles from Derwenthaugh to Redheugh (Gateshead), and

How Mill, looking northeast on 12 January 1957. Q6 0-8-0 No 63441 drifts down the track with a Blaydon-Carlisle goods train.
(Robert Leslie)

passengers were ferried across the Tyne to a temporary station in Newcastle at No. 66 The Close. The gap of about 10 miles between Blenkinsopp and Haydon Bridge was eventually completed, allowing the N&CR directors to travel between Redheugh and Carlisle (London Road) on 15 June 1838. The formal opening was on 18 June. This event was less than successful. Heavy rain drenched the passengers, and many were left shaken, and some injured, by two collisions.

The N&CR reached Newcastle via three miles of track and a temporary Tyne bridge. Formal opening to a station at the Shot Tower took place on 21 May 1839; regular services began on 21 October. The new Forth terminus opened on 1 March 1847. From 1 January 1851 the company used Central station, shared with the York, Newcastle & Berwick Railway. Although access to Carlisle Citadel had yet to be achieved, the 60¼-mile cross-country route was complete.

The N&CR eventually joined the NER empire on 17 July 1862. The Caledonian and Newcastle & Berwick railways had previously attempted to lease this strategic route. Although the latter, headed by George Hudson, persuaded the N&CR shareholders to favour his approach, and the YN&B leased the N&CR de facto from 1 August 1848, Hudson's disgrace and ruin in 1849 prevented the ratification of the lease in Parliament, and the N&CR regained independence. In May 1862 the NER negotiated entry of Newcastle trains into Carlisle Citadel station, and this took effect in 1864. London Road was relegated to goods use. In 1865-6, west of Haydon Bridge the NER replaced wooden river bridges with iron structures, involving minor route realignments. The 'temporary' single-track wooden bridge over the Tyne at Scotswood was replaced in 1870 with a double-track 6-span girder bridge. The NER ended the unconventional practice of right-hand running on the Newcastle-Carlisle route. Milton-Carlisle was re-signalled for left hand running in 1863, and the remainder in 1864. (In station descriptions that follow, 'up' and 'down' line refer to post-1864 arrangements.)

The Newcastle-Carlisle route left inhabitants of Newburn and Lemington, north of the Tyne, dependent upon Scotswood station. Although collieries in that area had waggonway access to the Tyne, a rail link was desirable for this traffic. On 16 June 1871 the **Scotswood, Newburn & Wylam Railway & Dock Company** Bill was successfully presented to Parliament, and the line opened from Scotswood to Newburn, with an intermediate station at Lemington, on 12 July 1875. The remainder opened to North Wylam on 13 May 1876, and in the following October the route was extended to join the Newcastle-Carlisle at West Wylam. Part of the 6½-mile route followed the course of the Wylam Waggonway. This section passed the cottage where George Stephenson was born; the proximity of this waggonway to his childhood home undoubtedly inspired his pioneering interest in railways. At each

end of the new line were engineering challenges. At Scotswood a ridge was to be crossed in a cutting, but, owing to geological difficulties, a short tunnel was excavated instead. At the west end, the graceful Wylam Bridge crossed the Tyne. Closely resembling Newcastle's Tyne Bridge, built 52 years later, Wylam Bridge was of wrought iron and had an 80yd arch from which the bridge floor was suspended on vertical ties. The dock in the company's title was not built because the Tyne was not dredged as far upstream as Scotswood, and was too shallow.

The new route effectively quadrupled the congested Scotswood-Prudhoe section, and some freight and passenger trains travelled its entire length, but until 1954 passenger trains from Newcastle generally terminated at North Wylam. In 1889 a complaint by a passenger, whose journey from Heddon-on-the-Wall involved a transfer with luggage between Wylam's stations (about ¼ mile) to travel to Prudhoe or beyond, failed to convince NER officials that passenger trains should operate west of North Wylam.

Train services
The Newcastle-Carlisle route is heavily used by passenger and freight traffic. From the earliest days coal, lead, timber, and livestock traffic were important. Excursions to such destinations as Gilsland Spa, Naworth Castle, and Hexham Abbey augmented regular passenger services. In 1849 five passenger trains ran each way on weekdays and two on Sunday, taking approximately three hours. Most trains stopped at all stations. In 1863 only four trains operated between Newcastle and Carlisle on weekdays (still with two on Sunday) but three extra services operated between Newcastle and Hexham. In 1920, the service had reached maturity. In the down direction there were ten Newcastle-Carlisle trains, mostly limited stop to Hexham, though one (the 12.40 am Irish boat train) ran non-stop, and two called at few intermediate stations. Naworth had the poorest service of any intermediate station. A further fifteen weekday and sixteen Saturday trains, generally calling at all stations, operated between Newcastle and Hexham, including two NBR services. Two Sunday trains ran from Newcastle to Carlisle and four more from Newcastle to Hexham. In summer 1964 the Newcastle-Carlisle line down train service had improved to thirteen Monday-Friday trains and seventeen on Saturday, including three summer-peak workings to Blackpool, Heads of Ayr, and Stranraer.

In 1920 ten trains operated each way on weekdays between Newcastle and North Wylam. By winter 1937-38 an intensive service of 32 weekday and 34 Saturday trains ran approximately half-hourly from Newcastle to North Wylam, whilst an hourly Sunday service from 1.20 to 10.20 pm called at all stations except Heddon-on-the-Wall. The weekday service halved in frequency by 1946; Sunday trains were little altered. In winter 1954-55 North Wylam's down

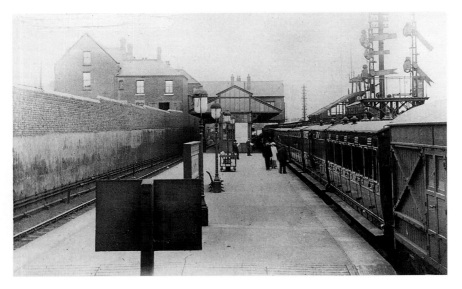

Even though it remained open until 1967, photographs of Elswick station are scarce. A down passenger train is seen at the single island platform c1905. *(Alan Young Collection)*

Scotswood, looking west in 1959. The lower, more distant pair of platforms on the left belong to the Blaydon line station. The higher pair, to the right, are on the North Wylam loop. *(Stations UK)*

Blaydon, looking east in 1959. The station was rebuilt by the NER in 1912 and was little altered until the early 1970s. *(Stations UK)*

service was reduced to only four weekday and three Saturday trains, but they all continued to Hexham. Sunday trains used the North Wylam loop in its final months, rather than calling at Blaydon and Wylam.

A minor route alteration was made on 27 May 1962 when Farnley Tunnel closed. It was replaced with a cutting, immediately south. The original single-track tunnel was reconstructed for double-track in 1845, but its condition deteriorated and about thirty years later reinforcement was needed that reduced clearances. Renewed deterioration caused BR to consider further reconstruction, but the cheaper option of diversion and cutting was adopted. The diversion reduced line curvature, so a 45mph restriction could be lifted, and future maintenance costs were reduced.

A more significant change occurred on 4 October 1982, when trains were diverted from Newcastle West Junction over King Edward Bridge, then via Norwood Junction and Dunston to Blaydon. This saved expenditure on maintaining Scotswood Bridge, and on points and crossings renewals at Blaydon and Newcastle West Junction. Tracks were removed from Scotswood Bridge, and the former line is now a one-mile siding from Newcastle. The diversion added four minutes to journey times. MetroCentre, adjacent to the new route, with its station opened in 1987, provides additional passenger traffic.

In winter 2002-03 the Newcastle to Carlisle service offers fifteen weekday and eleven Sunday trains, with a further fourteen (Monday-Friday) and twelve (Saturday) to Hexham. An intensive service of 22 trains (Monday-Saturday), and 31 on Sunday, terminates at MetroCentre. Sunday trains to MetroCentre began in 1994 when trading laws were relaxed. The Newcastle-Carlisle service is integrated into the wider network, origins and destinations of services including Morpeth, Saltburn, Whitehaven, and Stranraer. Amidst these improvements, minor stations, including Bardon Mill and Brampton, have suffered a reduced service since the early 1990s. Only three down and two up trains call at Blaydon on weekdays, whilst Dunston has one each way. The much-publicised reopening of Dunston in 1984 offered over twenty trains each way on weekdays! BR over-estimated the demand in an area well served by buses.

Branches and sidings

Passenger branches joined the Newcastle-Carlisle route, and they are individually described. There were freight branches and sidings too, notably near Newcastle, serving factories, collieries, power stations, and gasworks. Further west, branches served Stocksfield Creamery, Fourstones Quarries, Barcombe Colliery (Bardon Mill), quarries near Greenhead, and Carrick's creamery (Low Row). A mineral line connected Brampton Junction and Lambley. Warn (1976) describes a fascinating branch in Butstone valley, starting ½ mile east of Haltwhistle. In little over a mile it served two

woollen mills, a coke oven, brewery, corn mill, sawmill, coal depot, gas works, tile works, coal drops, and a colliery!

Motive power

As a 'secondary main line' with much passenger and goods traffic, the Newcastle-Carlisle route has hosted a variety of motive power and rolling stock. Services began with locomotives *Comet* (0-4-0) and *Rapid* (0-6-0), both built locally. The N&CR favoured six-coupled locomotives, some subsequently rebuilt into tanks to haul passenger stock. Absorption into the NER introduced a range of engines, some derived from other companies which, like the N&CR, it had absorbed. In time standardised NER designs appeared. By World War I classes C, P1, P2, P3, R, S, T2, and V provided most of the haulage. Under LNER administration Q class (4-4-0) ex-NER locomotives assumed many passenger duties. D49 (4-4-0), R(4-4-0) and V1 (2-6-2) were commonly seen, and East Coast main line Pacifics made occasional forays. In BR days ex-LNER classes continued to operate, with some appearances of ex-LMS and BR standard classes. The final days of steam-hauled goods saw classes K1, Q6, WD, and J27 locomotives at work. In 1958-9 change-over from loco-hauled passenger operation to diesel railcars occurred, classes 101 and 104 handling many duties. Goods haulage became the preserve of diesels too, including classes 40, 47 and, later, 60. Class 156 dmus operate many of today's passenger services.

Station architecture

This route has 'numerous stations of historic interest, possibly the oldest series retaining their original features that now exist in close proximity' (Biddle & Nock, 1983). The earliest railways were, of course, pioneers in providing stations. N&CR stations had no platforms, only a paved area between the house and the running lines. No shelters were provided for passengers, who probably huddled together in the stationmaster's front room, where tickets were also sold. At Blaydon, Hexham, Haydon Bridge, Greenhead, and Carlisle primitive ridge-and-furrow trainsheds, at right-angles to the tracks, and lacking screens, provided minimal shelter. Stations soon required upgrading to other companies' standards. In the 1850s platforms were added, leaving some buildings separate from the platforms (as at Bardon Mill and Greenhead). At other places (such as Riding Mill and Brampton Junction) platforms were inserted in front of the house, level with the window cills, requiring steps down to the house or offices.

There has been speculation regarding the architect of the early N&CR stations. Biddle (1973) suggested Benjamin Green. Research by Fawcett (2001) favours John Blackmore, who held a senior engineering post from the company's earliest days, and was latterly Chief Engineer. He possibly drew inspiration from popular architectural pattern books. However Corby crossing cottage, near

Wetheral, might have set the standard. This cottage was designed to satisfy Henry Howard, an N&CR director, through whose land the line passed. The original stations were of sandstone, generally single-storey with attic, some with a cross-gable window resting on wooden corbels. Windows were embellished with hood-moulds. Larger versions were at Hexham and Haltwhistle, whilst Stocksfield had a stone porch and Haydon Bridge and Wetheral each had a portico with Gothic arches. Waiting sheds were added in the 1850s. They typically possessed a stone back and sides, with a deep saw-tooth valance fronting the sloping roof. Their design is ascribed to Peter Tate, Blackmore's successor as Engineer-in-Chief. Some of these sheds survive in altered forms. In the same decade, Gilsland received an additional stone-built waiting room and a graceful glazed awning stretching the full length of the original and new buildings, to shelter patrons visiting the nearby spa. Wetheral, serving the Howard family, received a similar awning at the expense of the portico. Whilst part of Wetheral's awning survives, in 1902 the NER replaced that at Gilsland with an ungainly corrugated iron canopy, removed before closure. Some stations were rebuilt, including Scotswood after a fire in 1879, and Prudhoe (c 1880) and Blaydon (1912) with enlarged accommodation. Stations were added on the North Wylam loop (1875-81), at Elswick (1889) and Scotswood Works (1915). NER working timetables of 1878 indicate that a 'ticket platform' was located on the eastern approaches to Carlisle.

Station closures

Early closures were Warden and Allerwash (replaced by Fourstones in 1837), Brampton Fell (by 1850) and Blenkinsopp Hall Halt (1875). Carlisle's London Road terminus closed in 1864, when trains were diverted to Citadel. Passenger services between Blaydon and Redheugh were suspended in 1850, but resumed in 1852. However in 1853 they were abandoned east of Derwenthaugh, which retained a modest service until 1868. The 1866 Derwenthaugh service was limited to Saturday market trains, with three return workings from Newcastle, calling at Scotswood and Blaydon. Mickley, opened in 1859, had only market-day trains, and closed in 1915. The Dunston shuttle service from Newcastle began in 1909, but the General Strike (1926) caused its demise. Naworth closed in 1952; like its neighbours Low Row and How Mill (both closed in 1959), it served lightly populated countryside. Ryton (closed 1954) and Scotby (closed 1959) on the other hand, served large villages, but buses to Newcastle and Carlisle respectively offered a more frequent, convenient service. Bus competition also explains the closure, in 1958, of Lemington, Newburn, and Heddon-on-the-Wall.

The Transport Users' Consultative Committee Report, published on 18 February 1966, considered BR's proposal to close Elswick, Scotswood, Blaydon,

Blaydon station in April 1977. The façade of the building is in a sad state of disrepair. *(Alan Young)*

On 5 April 1977 a Newcastle-Hexham dmu enters the semi-derelict Blaydon station. Some months later the buildings were demolished and replaced with 'bus shelters'.

(Alan Young)

Wylam, Fourstones, Bardon Mill, Greenhead, Gilsland, Heads Nook, and Wetheral. Beeching (1963) recommended their closure, as well as Riding Mill and Corbridge (which were reprieved in autumn 1964). BR claimed that the proposed closures would allow accelerated dmu services - making them more attractive to the majority of users - and increase the dmu fleet's productivity by integrating these 'express' services with Newcastle-Hexham local workings. North Wylam, listed by Beeching for closure, was to remain open, whilst the Blaydon route would close. BR explained this decision, noting the expense of maintaining Scotswood Bridge; 'certain advantages' of the North Wylam route for freight working; declining business at Blaydon; and the ease of transferring Wylam's business 300yd to North Wylam. BR considered the retained stations 'fairly well placed strategically to attract people to use their cars to the stations and go forward on fast trains to their destinations'. There were numerous objections to the station closures (and the revised timetable), the case being strongest for Bardon Mill, Wylam, and Blaydon, the three that were eventually reprieved. Bardon Mill had 20 regular passengers, and the imminent closure of the local colliery was expected to encourage up to one hundred workers to use trains to travel to new jobs elsewhere. Eight passengers commuted between Wylam and Blaydon, and there was no alternative public transport. Although 75% of Blaydon's 107 regular passengers commuted to Newcastle, and

could use buses, the number was considered sufficient to retain the station. Buses would absorb Elswick's two regular users - commuters from Wylam and Hexham - despite the latter's claim that closure would increase the strain on road services. No-one challenged Greenhead's closure; the three known regulars were mothers travelling to Haltwhistle on Thursdays to a clinic. Cumberland Council did not oppose the closure of Wetheral (three regular users), but contested Heads Nook and Gilsland (just into Northumberland). 'The number of people using Heads Nook falls far short of justifying the station's existence' was BR's dismissal of the needs of the dozen passengers per day, five of whom were regular. Gilsland's closure attracted objections, some undoubtedly justified, others speculative or exaggerated. Claims that visitors to the convalescent home - the former spa - would be inconvenienced were dismissed because not a single visitor in 1965 had come by train. Likewise 'about fifteen teenagers' dependent on Saturday evening trains for entertainment in Carlisle were found, in BR's census, to be 'about three'! A protestor was aggrieved by the retention of Brampton Junction, 'nearly two miles from the town, used by virtually no passengers, and with half-hourly buses to Carlisle' while Gilsland was proposed for closure. BR responded that Brampton Junction was 'retained as a central point', but its future would depend on the level of use.

Trains between Scotswood and Prudhoe via

Wylam were suspended from 3 September 1966 for engineering work. They never again stopped at Scotswood's south platforms. The north platforms remained as notional railhead for the temporarily-closed Blaydon station, beyond the expected closure date in early January. Scotswood eventually closed in May 1967, when services via Blaydon were restored. Elswick, Fourstones, Greenhead, Gilsland, Heads Nook, and Wetheral closed in January 1967.

On the North Wylam loop, the apparently illogical decision was taken in 1958 to retain North Wylam, 300yd from Wylam station, whilst closing the other intermediates, where no alternative stations were available. However 1951 traffic statistics show that North Wylam was the busiest: 37,197 tickets were issued there, but under 25,000 for the other three stations combined. At that time, moreover, North Wylam was effectively a terminus with negligible traffic to or from the west. Its bookings exceeded those at Wylam (30,261). Because BR's proposal in 1966 to close Wylam but retain North Wylam was rejected, proceedings began in 1967 to close the North Wylam loop. North Wylam's annual passenger receipts of £4,650 outweighed operating costs of £2,100, but abandonment from North Stella (Newburn) to West Wylam Junction, including the bridge over the River Tyne, would save an estimated £8,500 in maintenance and renewal. Whereas BR emphasised the operating advantages of the North Wylam loop a year earlier, now, remarkably, its disadvantages emerged: North Wylam had speed restrictions owing to 'sharp curves, gradients, and poor foundations' (maximum gradient of 1 in 100) and would be expensive to upgrade to trunk route standards! Valiant protesters opposed the closure, including Northumberland County Council. Grounds for objection included the proximity of North Wylam to a planned housing estate; the unpleasant walk over the bridge to Wylam station in inclement weather; and the inconvenient layout and poor condition of that station. The TUCC Report of 12 September 1967 concluded that Wylam (population 1,495) did not warrant two stations, and that passengers used either station 'according to which particular train suits their immediate requirements'. On 11 March 1968 passenger traffic ceased on the loop and North Wylam closed. I travelled on two of the trains on Saturday 9 March (the penultimate day of service). There was a sense of 'business as normal' - no signs of impending doom such I noted on other lines so near to closure. Freight working had already ceased between North Stella, near Newburn, and West Wylam Junction on 14th September 1967. The junction with the Wylam-Prudhoe route was severed. Rails through North Wylam were retained until April 1972, when the line was cut back to Newburn. The Scotswood-Newburn section was taken out of use in December 1986. Most of the loop is a footpath (Tyne Riverside Country Park) with Stephenson's Cottage as a feature of interest.

Station modernisation

Except Hexham, the stations were de-staffed from 19 January 1969 - an economy BR had scorned three years earlier. A programme of modernisation of the stations began. Tall 'vandal-proof' electric lamp posts were installed in 1970-72, replacing gas lighting at Blaydon, Wylam, Prudhoe, Riding Mill, Corbridge, Hexham, and Haltwhistle, and oil lighting at Haydon Bridge, Bardon Mill, and Brampton Junction. (Prior to closure gas lighting was used at Scotswood, Newburn, Lemington, North Wylam, Wetheral, Scotby, and probably Elswick and Ryton. The others were oil lit.) Stocksfield, had electric lighting on LNER swan-neck standards, replaced in about 1963 with a bland BR design that survived until the 1980s. Haydon Bridge received BR corporate identity running-in boards and small nameplates in the 1960s. Blaydon, Prudhoe, Stocksfield, and Hexham had NE Region vitreous enamel running-in boards. All other stations had LNER wooden nameboards with raised lettering or flat, hand-painted boards, as at Haltwhistle and Bardon Mill. Totem signs were installed at Blaydon, Prudhoe, Stocksfield, Riding Mill, Hexham, and North Wylam. By 1974, corporate identity signs were found at all stations. Demolition of buildings took place at Prudhoe (1973) and Blaydon (1977); Brampton's main building disappeared soon after. 'Bus shelters' were added in their place. Bardon Mill has been remodelled, a standard arrangement replacing staggered platforms.

Station-by-station

Elswick, a populous industrial suburb of Newcastle, received a station in 1889. Its 25ft-wide island platform had a glazed awning supported by iron columns and spandrels with the Star of David motif - as at Heaton (1887). The offices were above the up line. In 1895 more tickets were issued than at any other Carlisle line intermediate station, except Blaydon. For many years Elswick was a 'ticket platform' where passengers' tickets on Newcastle-bound trains were collected. Situated close to Scotswood Road, Elswick suffered from tram and bus competition, yet remained heavily used until the 1930s. In the 1950s traffic declined. Sunday trains ceased to call in 1952 and, from 11 September 1961, it was unstaffed. The following year the awnings were demolished. In its final years the station was a sorry sight, the weed-infested platform boasting only decapitated lamp posts and one illegible nameboard. It closed in 1967, and the platform was soon demolished. Track realignment removed all traces of the station.

Scotswood Works Halt, about 700yd east of Scotswood station, opened in World War I for workers at Armstrong Whitworth's munitions factory. It was built at that company's expense following an Agreement with the NER of 25 August 1915. The 150yd island platform was reached by a footbridge. Because of the volume of traffic Armstrong Whitworth and the Ministry of Munitions paid for the halt to be enlarged. A platform, 150yd long and 10-14ft wide, was added south of the down line. The island platform became the up platform, fenced on its southern side. Shelters were installed centrally on both platforms, that on the up platform being larger. The new platform was used from 30 May 1919. The layout thus had two platforms facing in the same direction - an unusual arrangement, also found at West Auckland (County Durham). The train service was intensive, as shown in the November 1918 working timetable. (The halt did not appear in public timetables.) On weekdays between 5.30 and 7.00 am twelve trains called (eight of them workmen's trains - not publicly advertised). Four trains were from Newcastle, three from Scotswood, and one each from Hexham, North Wylam, Newburn, and Lintz Green. A further service ran from Blackhill for workmen, but its advertised origin was Lintz Green. On Saturday four calls were made between noon and 1.00 pm. On Monday-Friday evenings, trains to a variety of destinations made fifteen calls between 4.00 and 7.00 pm; the majority, again, were workmen's trains. The 5.08 pm to Newcastle actually started at the halt. Seven trains called on Sunday between 4.15 and 7.00 pm.

The Agreement with the NER to operate the halt expired at the close of World War I, but Armstrong Whitworth requested its retention, subject to one month's notice of discontinuation by themselves or the NER. The workforce declined, and Armstrong Whitworth approached the LNER (successor to the NER) to end the service on 27 September 1924. Armstrong Whitworth acquired the government's interests in the platform and buildings and offered to sell them to the LNER who could then dismantle them. The halt closed, but reopened from April 1941 until 1944, again serving muntions workers. It was eventually demolished in 1948 - only to appear for the first time on the One-inch Ordnance Survey map in 1953!

Scotswood's two platforms, on the Newcastle-Blaydon line, possibly opened in 1839. The northern Newburn line pair was added in 1875. Curving away from the original platforms, they were at a higher level, and ended some 50yd to the east. The original station buildings burned down on 17 October 1879. Tickets were then temporarily issued from the signal box. By the mid-1880s new buildings, including waiting sheds, were completed, and the two sets of platforms were connected by bridge and subway. The new station building, at the east end of the southernmost platform, was an unassuming brick structure with a small awning. It was accompanied by a wooden pitched-roof building. A similar wooden structure accommodated office and waiting facilities on the opposite platform. Two further, equally unimposing, wooden buildings served the northern platforms. Sidings and warehouses were west of the Newburn line platforms and at the east end of the down Blaydon line platform.

Scotswood was busy until the 1930s, but buses drained much of its traffic. 144,462 tickets were issued in 1895, but only 17,180 in 1951. When I requested a ticket to Scotswood at Newcastle Central in 1966, the clerk recommended that I catch a bus instead because they were more frequent! With such lukewarm support, even from their own staff, is it surprising that BR suburban stations failed to attract passengers? When the Blaydon route temporarily closed in September 1966 (for works connected with the new Scotswood road bridge) the southern platforms fell out of use. Complete closure came in May 1967. Scotswood's buildings and platforms were demolished within five years.

Dunston-on-Tyne (formerly County Durham) had a shuttle service from Newcastle beginning in January 1909. The island platform was reached by a ramp from the road over-bridge. On the platform was an unpretentious, lengthy single-storey brick building, surrounded by a shallow awning. In 1910 'autocars' provided ten Newcastle-Dunston trains per day each way, calling also at Gateshead West. The service was suspended from 1 May 1918 until 1 October 1919, and again on 4 May 1926, but it was not resumed. The buildings were dismantled, but the platform was retained. It was demolished to make way for a new, slightly shorter, version when Dunston re-opened in 1984. At first the restored train service was frequent, but it has dwindled to one down departure in the morning and one up in the afternoon on weekdays - a minimal entitlement that fulfils Network Rail's obligation to provide a service.

MetroCentre station has two platforms and pedestrian access to the shopping centre. Shelters are provided on each platform. It opened as Gateshead MetroCentre in 1987; 'Gateshead' was dropped from May 1993. Although most shoppers reach the mall by road, an intensive train service is operated.

Blaydon (formerly Co Durham). The original station had a small, single-storey building, and narrow platforms; a primitive trainshed was provided in the early days, but, later, a crude but lengthy platform shelter accompanied the station building. In 1912 the station was reconstructed on a grander scale. Most of the new tall, single-storey structure on the south side was red brick. 97yd glazed awnings of ridged cross-section covered much of the two platforms. They ended with glazed screens and were supported by iron columns and spandrels of a hooped design, as at West Jesmond (opened 1900). A covered footbridge linked the platforms. The exterior possessed restrained dignity. The lofty central section carried a pavilion roof. Its segmental-arched openings were separated by four sandstone pilasters that rose above the eaves, and were capped by large ball-finials. A cross-gable window concealed and lit the footbridge, and was complemented by dormer-style ventilators on either side. The up platform had an unremarkable single-storey building with a pitched roof, flanked by high walls.

Ryton, Co Durham. An undated view, looking west.
(Alan Young Collection)

Wylam, looking towards Carlisle in April 1976. The station buildings and the elevated signal box enjoy 'listed' status.　*(Alan Young)*

Prudhoe, looking west in about 1970. The buildings were demolished in 1973.
(Lens of Sutton)

Stocksfield, looking east on 30 December 1961. A standard NER footbridge spans the tracks. Note the N&CR waiting shed, also the early-NER building beyond, containing the booking office and a waiting room.
(Geoffrey C Lewthwaite)

Riding Mill, looking west in 1937. The track-level building on the extreme left dates from the station's opening in 1835; the platform was added in front of it some years later.
(Stations UK)

Corbridge on a fine, frosty afternoon in December 1991. The building, which has Grade II listed status, is unlike any other on the Newcastle-Carlisle line. *(Alan Young)*

After de-staffing in 1969, the awnings were dismantled. The lengthy wall on the north platform, built purely to carry an awning, looked ungainly and attracted local graffiti artists. Vandals smashed what was breakable; an arsonist attempted to destroy what remained. In *Off the Rails* (1977), the companion booklet to the Save Britain's Heritage exhibition of endangered railway architecture, I contributed a 'Demolished and Maltreated Stations' chapter. I remarked that Blaydon was probably Britain's least attractive station. Local television and newspapers seized upon this and insisted on action to rectify matters. BR's response was, rather than repair the buildings, to bulldoze them later that year and install 'bus shelters'. The formerly busy station, issuing over quarter-of-a-million tickets, and at which almost every train called, now has only a token service. It is poorly sited to serve a town with excellent bus links.

Blaydon had extensive sidings, handling Newcastle-Carlisle derived traffic, also waggons from the East Coast main line (via Derwenthaugh), the Derwent Valley, local collieries, and other businesses. An engine shed existed from early N&CR days, but a larger one opened in 1900 for goods and passenger locomotives. In 1930, 84 locomotives were based there. Under BR, shed 52C bade farewell to steam locomotives in March 1963, and closed two years later.

Ryton (formerly Co. Durham) village is over 100ft above the River Tyne. Residents had to negotiate a steep lane to reach their riverside station. For many years they willingly undertook this walk; 144, 826 tickets were issued in 1914. The two facing platforms were linked by a subway. The house, stone-built and with two pitched roofs aligned west-to-east, was on the up platform. Extending forward to the platform was a cumbersome wooden structure with waiting and office accommodation, decorated with a huge saw-tooth valance. At the east end of the opposite platform was a standard deep-valanced wooden building containing waiting rooms, and a separate booking shed near the subway entrance. In the 1920s frequent bus services began, and villagers spurned their station. Bookings tumbled to 14,227 in 1937, and 2,685 in 1951. Closure came in 1954. By the early-1960s it was demolished. Only small goods were handled at Ryton; larger items were dealt with at Blaydon.

Wylam is marginally in Northumberland. Its charming station retains a Victorian atmosphere, despite intrusive lamp standards and modern signing. The house stands at track level on the south side, east of the level crossing. This original 1835 building is possibly the oldest at any functioning British station - thus its Grade II* listed status. The neo-Tudor house has the distinctive cross-gable upper window projecting on corbels. It was sympathetically extended in 1897 when the outside walls were raised to create a full upper floor. The down platform, added immediately east of the house, has a single-storey extension, built at an early date. This is also stone-built, with its roof hipped at the eastern end. It formerly contained waiting accommodation (partly open-fronted), toilets, and offices. Its east end is slightly recessed, providing a shelter supported by columns. A booking office window was installed in the east end of the house. West of the crossing are the listed gantry-mounted signal box and the up platform. This had a wooden waiting shed, removed by BR and replaced with a 'bus shelter'. A footbridge, differing from the standard NER design, with close-set diamond lattice parapets, connects the platforms.

Prudhoe has conventional facing platforms east of the level crossing. Since 1973 'bus shelters' have provided the passenger accommodation. There was formerly a brick-built single-storey building on the up platform in the twin pavilion style of about 1880, resembling that at Bensham. A timber-fronted verandah was enclosed by the projecting wings. On the opposite platform was a small pent-roofed wooden waiting shed. The station was renamed Prudhoe for Ovingham: lengthy LNER boards carried this name. Timetables from 1972 abbreviated the name to Prudhoe.

Mickley opened in 1859 to serve the hamlet of Eltringham, a brick and tile works, a colliery, and coke ovens. Mickley village was 3/4 mile away and 300ft higher than the station. A small building stood on the up platform, with a signal box at the west end. The down platform might have been without buildings. Trains appear to have been limited to Hexham and Newcastle market days. In August 1866 there was only one Saturday passenger train, which travelled from Newcastle to Mickley and back in mid-afternoon. In June 1877 one Saturday call in each direction was supplemented by another each way on alternate Saturdays; presumably local people knew *which* alternate Saturdays! Only 826 tickets were issued in 1895. In 1907 this had risen to 5,070 - still a tiny figure for that time. In 1910 a more generous Saturday service was offered, and one train each way on Tuesday allowing a visit to Hexham market. In late-1914, a landslip required the tracks to be slewed across the south platform's site while the ground was stabilised, and rebuilding of the platform was presumably thought unnecessary. Mickley disappeared from the timetable in June 1915.

Stocksfield had an interesting layout and attractive buildings. The original house was single-storey with an attic, and possessed a tall, pitched roof and triple chimney stacks. A stone entrance porch faced the rails. The building was separated from the later down platform's eastern ramp by a goods siding. This platform, which sliced through a corner of the goods shed, had a typical N&CR deep-valance waiting shed with an open front. The up platform was staggered slightly eastwards and, towards its eastern end, had a further waiting shelter with its awning carried forward on columns. There was also a single-storey office building added by the NER to complement the house. It included a V-shape bay window with a high parapet. Sadly this building is no more. A typical NER footbridge was provided. In addition to installing vitreous enamel nameboards and totems, BR emblazoned the valances of the shelters with 'British Railways Stocksfield' in huge white letters on a tangerine background. Dismayed by the neglect of their station after de-staffing, local residents assumed responsibility for tending the garden. It remains a pleasant place to wait for a train.

Riding Mill has much rural charm, although firmly within Newcastle's commuter zone. The original Tudoresque house, partially obscured by the down platform, has a corbel-supported cross-gable window. On close inspection, evidence of awkward additions and alterations (from 1871 and 1913) can be seen, but the building is still attractive. The typical NER footbridge remains in place. An open front timber waiting shelter with deep valance stood on the down platform, and timber-and-glass waiting rooms on the up platform. These facilities were removed by the early-1970s. Now there are simple, curved-roofed shelters on each platform. Other points of interest were the slightly staggered platforms, and the barrow crossing that interrupted the down platform in line with the western up platform ramp. This gap in the platform was covered with sleepers, when not in use.

Corbridge station is across the Tyne and almost a mile south of the village. The original building was probably on the down platform, but in 1847 construction of the (A68) bridge required its demolition. Its replacement, on the up platform

immediately east of the bridge, was a sober two-storey house, its platform verandah carried on Tuscan columns. This building survives in commercial use. The former gantry signal box burned down in about 1960 when sparks from an engine ignited birds' nests in the structure. West of the road bridge the up platform adjoined the goods shed and had a passenger shelter which, for some years, had 'British Railways Corbridge' painted on the valance. By 1972 the goods shed and shelter were removed and a BR metal-and-glass 'bus shelter' had appeared. Both platforms now have more imaginative shelters. The iron footbridge, directly west of the overbridge, resembled that at Wylam.

Hexham, the principal intermediate station, possessed a house with office and waiting room. This elegant building included an upper storey with a cross-gabled window placed above a ground-floor bay on the eastern elevation. An early trainshed survived until the 1870s, chained down in later years to prevent it from blowing away! When Hexham became the junction for Border Counties and Allendale, its accommodation proved inadequate. The station building was therefore extended, and conventional platforms were installed in 1871. Glazed awnings and end-screens were added to both through platforms. The wider awning, adjoining the buildings on the down platform, is supported by a double row of branching iron columns - a design used at Durham and Selby. The awning opposite, backed by a plain

Hexham, looking southeast. A class 101 dmu calls on 22 July 1984. *(Alan Young)*

Fourstones, looking west in July 1966.

(Gordon Biddle Collection)

wall, has a single row of columns. At one time a further awning sheltered the exterior. An iron footbridge (formerly enclosed) connects the platforms. Bay platforms were provided behind the up platform and at the western end of the down platform, beyond the buildings. West signal box on the up platform was tall enough to have a clear view over the adjacent road bridge. This box has been removed, but the listed gantry-mounted East box remains in use. Until 1991, Hexham had goods facilities, largely east of the station. The goods shed survives. This N&CR building has a ridge-and-furrow roof. There was also a small locomotive shed. The original was destroyed by fire in 1929, and its replacement was used until 1959. In 1947 its allocation was six locomotives. Hexham station is staffed and beautifully maintained: a superb floral display appears in summer. Part of the building is used as a café.

Warden and **Allerwash** were replaced by **Fourstones**, midway between them, in 1837.

Fourstones original station house, set back from the up line, was a dignified, single-storey affair. It had a T-plan with a large, round bay facing the track. Fawcett suggests that the distinctive style was chosen because this station was used by John Clayton, legal advisor to the N&CR and Newcastle's Town Clerk. In 1880, when new facilities were constructed a little to the east, the waiting shed on the down platform was retained. The new building was of the NER's favoured single-storey twin-pavilion layout, built of stone, with bay windows on each pavilion. Fourstones was a truly

delightful country station. In summer passengers enjoyed the sight and fragrance of climbing roses that adorned the platform fences. After closure (1967) the platforms and buildings survived for several years before demolition. The original house remains in residential use.

Haydon Bridge, a temporary terminus from 1836-8, had a smart, single-storey building, with a hipped roof. A small triple-arched porch faced the tracks. The N&CR installed an open-fronted waiting shed on the up platform. In 1877 new buildings were provided on the down platform. The house was a dour two-storey structure. To its west, offices and waiting rooms were in a single-storey twin-pavilion building, resembling earlier versions at the Scotswood-Blackhill stations. It had a verandah between the wings and a gabled bay at the west end. Close-by was a water-crane. There was no footbridge; passengers used a sleeper crossing at the west end. The original building survived until at least 1965. The passenger buildings on the down platform were removed after 1972, leaving only the station house facing the N&CR waiting shed. By 1989 a new shelter was in use on the down platform.

Bardon Mill was another early station, originally without platforms. On the north side the house was remote from the running line, and the up platform was later constructed some 50yd east. The house, still occupied, is an appealing two-storey structure notable for a first-storey bay facing the tracks, and tall chimneystacks. Between the house and platform, the NER added office accommodation in a long, wooden

Haydon Bridge, looking east in about 1970. The austere buildings on the right were constructed by the NER in 1876. The British Rail corporate identity nameboard and elderly oil lanterns are somewhat incongruous neighbours. *(Lens of Sutton)*

A Newcastle to Carlisle dmu calls at the new westbound platform at Bardon Mill on 1 May 1982. *(Martin Bairstow)*

On 10 April 1972 two class 101 dmus stand at Haltwhistle's island platform. To the right a Newcastle-Carlisle working calls at 11.30, connecting with the 12.00 for Alston. Posts have been installed for electric lighting to replace the gas lamps. *(Alan Young)*

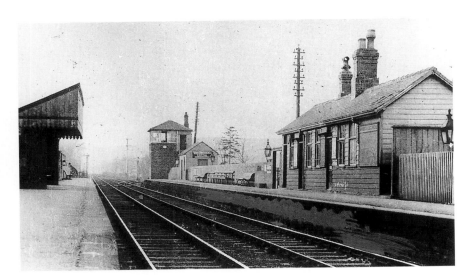

Greenhead, looking northwest before 1914
(Alan Young Collection)

Gilsland, looking northeast. The large awning on the left, installed by the NER, was dismantled before the station closed.
(Alan Young Collection)

Gilsland in August 2001. The platform has gone, but the buildings on the up side of the tracks remain. The older structure on the right is the characteristic Newcastle & Carlisle Railway cottage, to which rather unattractive dormers have been added.
(Alan Young)

shed. This building remains in good repair. On the up platform a typical N&CR waiting shed survives, but hideously altered. A sleeper crossing connected the western ramp of the up platform to the eastern ramp of the down platform. A smaller version of the office building was found here, providing waiting accommodation. The signal box was west of the down platform. The down platform has been demolished; its replacement, in timber, is opposite the up platform.

Haltwhistle's importance was acknowledged in the relatively large house, built north of the tracks. It boasted a bay window and groups of fine chimneystacks. A westward extension contained offices. There was originally a paved area between the house and running line, fenced to prevent 'unprincipled persons' unauthorised access to the trains: a similar arrangement existed at Hexham. The up platform was added east of the house, with a wooden shed providing enclosed waiting accommodation. The down platform was actually an island, staggered to face the station house. Alston trains used its southern side. A long, wooden shed contained waiting rooms. At the eastern end of this platform were a wooden signal box on a brick base, constructed in 1901 (both sides overhanging a narrow base because of space restrictions), and an NER footbridge. A water tank, goods shed and sidings were on the up side west of the main building, with further sidings on the down side. Something of Haltwhistle's appeal was lost when the Alston branch closed, but the station retains much of interest. The main building is in well maintained, part of it used as an information office. The platform buildings, signal box, footbridge, water tower, and even sidings are *in situ.* The signal box was decommissioned in 1993 when colour light signalling was introduced. A new prefabricated building on the up side replaced it

Blenkinsopp Hall Halt was private and fell out of use in 1875. The single-storey gate lodge-cum-crossing house, with prominent gable-end finials, stands at the entrance to the grounds of the Hall.

Greenhead, like other N&CR stations, had an unconventional layout. The house, set back from the up track, was of the two-storey variety with a cross-gable window, and was extended in the 1870s. In 1888 office functions moved into a wooden shed on the platform that also contained waiting rooms and toilets. The down platform's most prominent structure was a tall, hipped-roof building accommodating cottages, entered at first floor level from the adjacent road. There was also an N&CR waiting shed. After World War II Greenhead was lightly used. Only 739 tickets were issued in 1951, and its train service was limited, yet it escaped closure until 1967. The platforms, waiting shed and up platform buildings were soon demolished, but the house survives, as does the tall building on the down side. The former engine shed, on the up side, is of particular interest: it is probably the oldest surviving example in Britain!

Gilsland (Rose Hill until 1869) was in a village straddling the border with Cumberland. It formerly served a spa, later converted into a convalescent home. The original building was set back from the up track. This gap proved advantageous when a platform was built: it was broad enough to handle large numbers of passengers using excursion trains to visit the spa, and could accommodate an elegant awning to shelter them. The house was in the N&CR Tudor style. Its cross-gable window was corbelled-out and had a steep raised gable. The NER inserted a booking-office window, facing the platform. In 1910 the house was enlarged with the addition of crudely designed dormers. This unfortunate addition was obscured by the equally crass corrugated iron platform roofing that, in 1902, replaced the earlier verandah. In its favour this 26ft 6in-span structure with a partial end-screen could shelter more passengers! Southwest of the house the N&CR added a separate office and waiting room, also of stone, to complement the original structure. The NER added a further pitched-roof wooden office building at the northeast end. On the facing down platform were a signal box and a stone pent-roof waiting shed, its front of wood and glass. Both were of NER provenance. The platform roof was removed long before the station closed. The columns that carried it remained as robust posts for oil lanterns. In 1907 Gilsland issued 20,710 tickets, but excursions brought many more passengers through its doors. By 1951 only 1,494 tickets were sold, and excursion visits were few since the spa had closed. After trains ceased to call in 1967 the platforms and down shelter were dismantled, but the up-side buildings are extant.

Low Row served an adjacent hamlet and scattered farms. The 1836 house was beside the down track, northeast of the level crossing. It featured the familiar cross-gable corbelled-out window. A two-storey addition was made to the southeast, whilst a single-storey platform building was added to the southwest. The NER installed wooden buildings on both platforms. Each contained a booking office and waiting accommodation with sliding doors, whilst the longer down platform building included toilets. North of the through lines, goods facilities were provided for Naworth Coal Company and, to the south, from 1921 a siding served a creamery. Never a busy station - 6,482 tickets were issued in 1911-passenger services ceased in 1959, followed by goods in 1965. The house survives, in residential use.

Naworth was provided for the Earl of Carlisle of Naworth Castle; the station opened to the public in 1871. The house was on the up side, northeast of the level crossing. The substantial two-storey section had N&CR hood-moulds on the lower windows and two cross-gable upper windows facing the rails. There was a single-storey extension to the northeast. The down platform faced this building whilst the up platform was southwest of the

Low Row, seen from a Blackburn-Gateshead MetroCentre excursion on 19 November 1988. The building shows clear evidence of its Newcastle & Carlisle Railway origin, despite some alterations. *(Alan Young)*

Naworth, looking north east. It began life as a private station for the Earl of Carlisle, and regular passenger services were handled from 1871 until 1952.
(Alan Young Collection)

When viewed from a Largs-Newcastle train on 17 August 1974, Brampton Junction still retained its curious assemblage of buildings.
(Alan Young)

Heads Nook, looking east c1900. The facilities on the platforms were somewhat basic.
(Alan Young Collection)

D20 4-4-0 No 62371 passing Wetheral with a Carlisle to Newcastle semi-fast.
(Martin Bairstow Collection)

Scotby (LNER) about 1939, with a westbound J39.
(Alan Young Collection)

crossing. Small wooden sheds stood on each platform. There were no goods facilities. Excursions brought passengers to Naworth Castle, but otherwise traffic was light. In 1907 only 4,524 tickets were issued. After closure in 1952, the platforms and sheds were soon removed.

Brampton Junction. In 1836 a station named Milton opened 1½ miles from Brampton. (The Brampton Railway provided a horse-drawn service into the town.) The house was on the down side, near the northeast end of the added platform, whilst a pair of tiny cottages was constructed a few yards southwest. By 1883 extensions had been added to the house in both directions along the platform, incorporating the cottages. The house itself had been enlarged, with dormer windows flanking the earlier cross-gable window. A short-lived glazed awning was installed in front of the house and extensions. The platform was raised to cill level on the original house. On the facing island platform, the NER added a pent-roof wooden waiting shed, enclosed at the front, with saw-tooth valances to the front and sides. Brampton Town trains used the northwest face of this platform. In 1870 Milton was renamed Brampton Junction. The suffix 'Junction' lasted until 1971 -almost fifty years after passengers had changed trains for Brampton Town! LNER 'Brampton Jct' nameboards survived until at least 1977. For many years, Brampton Junction was busy; 28,715 tickets were issued in 1907. Excursions brought passengers to visit the nearby beauty-spot, Talkin Tarn. Custom dramatically declined when buses began to ply between Brampton and Carlisle, and in 1967 only 1,979 passengers were booked. By 1977, on the down platform, only the northeast extension to the original building remained, with the water tower behind it. In 2001 only a 'bus shelter' was provided, whilst the shed on the up platform had suffered unsightly alterations, the fenestration replaced with boarding and a tiny entrance. The NER footbridge is still used. A long-closed signal box remains northeast of the platforms.

Brampton Junction (Milton) was the birthplace of the 'Edmondson' cardboard railway ticket that was standard in Britain until the 1960s. In August 1837, Thomas Edmondson, the booking clerk, installed a small printing press to add dates to tickets he had already printed, numbered sequentially, and stacked in racks. The new system allowed the number of tickets sold and money collected to be checked easily, and the N&CR adopted it at all stations to replace their unwieldy accounting system. Edmondson left the N&CR in 1839, having been 'head-hunted' by the Manchester & Leeds Railway.

Brampton Fell, according to Clinker's *Register,* had a passenger service until 1850. The delightful N&CR single-storey building, with its massive chimneystack, is still in residential use.

How Mill served the village of Hayton. The house, on the up side west of the level crossing, is extant. The platforms were staggered, with the up platform east of the crossing and the down platform to the west. There were formerly wooden waiting sheds on the platforms, with the booking hall in a separate shed at the entrance to the up platform. An NER signal box stood on the down side east of the crossing. In 1907, 14,779 tickets were issued, falling to 2,890 in 1951 - somewhat more than Gilsland and Greenhead which outlived How Mill. Passenger and goods services ended in 1959, and the platforms were soon removed.

Heads Nook opened in 1862. In 1863 it appeared as a timetable footnote, with two services calling daily (including Sunday) in each direction. The platforms were in a cutting, with the rather plain station house above the southeast (down) platform. This platform had a pent-roofed waiting shed of stone and timber, whilst a pitched-roofed wooden shed stood on the up platform. In 1907, 18,368 tickets were issued, but only 2,471 in 1951. Goods services were withdrawn in 1965, and passenger services in 1967. The down platform and buildings survived for several years. In 2001 the house remained in use, and fragments of the platforms could be seen.

Wetheral stands immediately west of the viaduct over the River Eden gorge. It is in a deep cutting and on a curve, tight enough to require check-rails. The 1836 building, on the up side and adjacent to the end of the viaduct, was single-storey with a triple-arch porch. A taller, single-storey building was added to its western side, with a further two-storey house to the north. The N&CR provided a glazed verandah in front of the single-storey buildings. The up platform ramp is a little west of these buildings. On the up platform the NER added a brick and timber shed, with numerous windows. The down platform also had a waiting shed. The signal box was on the cutting side, above the down platform. A goods dock was west of the station, but Wetheral's main facilities were at Corby Gates, beyond the viaduct. A footway to Corby was on the north side of the viaduct, which members of the public could use for a halfpenny fee, but the charge was waived for pedestrians going to or from church services or choir practice in Wetheral! The station is conveniently situated to serve Wetheral village. In 1907 trade was brisk: 43,729 tickets were issued. Buses lured the passengers away, and in 1951 issues fell to only 1,104. Nevertheless passenger trains called until 1967, goods traffic having ceased in 1955. The station was left almost intact after closure. The up platform shed and the buildings huddled at the end of viaduct were in good order; part of the N&CR verandah remained. In 1977 an LNER nameboard was in place, and gas lamps adorned the footbridge and the access to the footway over the viaduct. Following pressure from residents in the expanding village, the passenger service was restored in 1981. Few changes were needed to the station. Whereas in earlier years BR might have demolished the buildings and installed 'bus shelters', sensitivity was shown. An attractive brick shelter, with a curved roof and saw-tooth valance, was constructed on the down platform.

Lemington, looking west, c1910. A Throckley-bound tram on Scotswood Road is crossing the bridge over the railway.
(Alan Young Collection)

Newburn, looking west from the level crossing, in NER days. *(Alan Young Collection)*

North Wylam, looking west in 1951. Although it was a through station, for almost eighty years trains from Newcastle usually terminated here. Wylam station, on the Blaydon route, was only 300 yards away.
(Locomotive & General Railway Photographs)

The LNER nameboard was retained. New electric lighting was less intrusive than at other Newcastle-Carlisle stations.

Scotby's red sandstone station house, recessed from the up running line, was of the N&CR cross-gable style. Extensions and alterations greatly transformed it. On the up platform the NER constructed a standard timber building for booking and waiting facilities. The N&CR shelter, on the down platform, had a booking office in one corner. In 1889 it was replaced with a wooden structure containing an office, waiting room, and toilets. It was later extended to include a ticket collector's room. Being close to Carlisle, bus competition was intense. 24,792 tickets were issued in 1911, but only 506 in 1951. The station survived until 1959, closing simultaneously to goods and passengers. The platforms and their buildings survived for several years. The house is in residential use. (Scotby also had a station on the Settle & Carlisle Railway. It closed in 1942, but the typical Midland Railway building is still standing.)

Carlisle London Road was the western terminus until 1863, when the NER gained access to Citadel station. Thereafter only goods traffic was handled. In 1881 it was largely demolished when a new goods depot was constructed. The handsome two-storey N&CR building had a pitched roof, at right angles to the tracks, ending with raised gables and a ground floor bay. Single-storey wings projected from the main structure. One of the N&CR's detached trainsheds with a ridge-and-furrow roof afforded some shelter to passengers.

Lemington and the other North Wylam loop stations were architecturally uninspired. Here, the house was a dull, substantial brick structure. Both platforms had pitched-roof wooden buildings. Road transport - first trams then buses - passed the station, and the 78,465 bookings in 1911 fell to 12,799 by 1951. Passenger services ended in 1958 and goods in 1960, then the station was swiftly demolished. (From 17 June 1963 until 7 July 1964 Lemington reopened as a coal depot.)

Newburn was west of the level crossing on a tight curve. The platform buildings were as unpretentious as those at Lemington. The up platform had a range of wooden buildings, with only one on the down platform, reflecting the need to provide facilities for Newcastle-bound passengers rather than for the few to Heddon-on-the-Wall or North Wylam. A non-standard iron footbridge on brick piers bisected the platforms, and, with the tall NER signal box at the crossing, was the station's dominant feature. Newburn suffered more than Lemington from road transport competition. Bookings tumbled from 106,798 in 1911 to 9,537 in 1951. After closure to passengers in 1958, goods facilities survived until 1965. The platforms were demolished in the mid-1960s.

Heddon-on-the-Wall was added in 1881. The two 100yd platforms were staggered either side of a level crossing. The buildings were close to the crossing. The up platform (east of the crossing) had two adjoining wooden buildings, both typical of the NER style in favour at that time. The smaller western one was a waiting shed, and the larger building contained the booking office and a further waiting room. Another waiting shed was on the down platform. Lemington Colliery waggonway, north of the running lines, was slewed northwards to accommodate the up platform. Although used by colliery workers, the valley-floor station was inconvenient for the village, over a mile away along a steep track. In 1911, 14,124 tickets were issued, but only 2,428 in 1951; by the 1950s many of Heddon's residents were probably unaware that they had a station! It closed entirely in 1958 and was soon demolished.

North Wylam had two 130yd platforms. Acknowledging its greater importance than its neighbours and *de facto* terminus status, North Wylam had brick buildings, but they were dull, single-storey structures. The main one on the down platform contained (from west to east) a porters' room, booking and parcels office, general and ladies' waiting rooms, and a lamp-room with gentlemen's toilet behind. A signal box was on the platform, east of the building. The up platform had a pent-roofed enclosed waiting shed and toilet. Goods facilities were south of the main building. A concrete footbridge joined the ensemble in about 1960. North Wylam closed in 1968. In the previous year 34,698 tickets were sold, the figure inflated by the temporary closure of Wylam during 1967. When the rails were removed in 1972 the station was still substantially intact. However it has now disappeared completely.

This cottage was George Stephenson's birthplace. It stands on the north side of the former railway - now lifted and converted into a footpath - between North Wylam and Heddon-on-the-Wall. *(Peter E Baughan Collection)*

A Metro-Cammell diesel multiple unit, bound for Newcastle, passing the up platform of Heddon-on-the-Wall. Note the splendid LNER nameboard. *(E E Smith / N E Stead Collection)*

Class B1 4-6-0 No 61219 of Carlisle Canal shed hauling a Carlisle-Newcastle train over Wylam Bridge on 14 April 1952. *(J W Armstrong Trust)*

The Allendale Branch

Langley, c1900. An Allendale-Hexham train is about to collect a large number of passengers.
(Courtesy J. Torday / The Garden Station)

From Hexham (Border Counties Junction) this 12 mile 25ch branch climbed from the Tyne valley through sparsely populated uplands, to Catton in the East Allen Valley. It was built as an outlet for lead smelters that thrived in the mid-19th Century. From 1835, Haydon Bridge station on the Newcastle-Carlisle railway provided a link to the outside world. Lead, mined in the local hills and smelted at Allenheads, Langley, or near Allendale Town, was conveyed along cart tracks to the station. However, as foreign competition grew, a cheaper means of transporting the metal was sought. The first attempt to provide rail access failed; in 1846 Parliament rejected the Wear Valley Extension Railway's proposal to link Frosterley (Weardale) and Alston, with a branch to Allenheads. In the 1850s major local lead producers and landowners campaigned for rail access, to enable metal to be exported efficiently, and suitable coal to be brought to the smelters from Tyneside. The Hexham & Allendale Railway route was surveyed in 1864. It received Royal Assent on 19 June 1865. The enabling Act permitted the Allendale Town to Allenheads section to be omitted if financial or other problems were encountered. The North Eastern Railway was enthusiastic, subscribing £10,000 to the initial cost.

The Engineer, Thomas J Bewick, faced the task of taking the railway from approximately 150ft to almost 800ft across hilly terrain. Much of the single-track route required cuttings or embankments, and curves as tight as 15ch radius. Trains would face a punishing gradient of up to 1 in 50 for the 7¾ miles from Border Counties Junction to Langley. A similar climb confronted trains from the southern terminus to Staward. The route was chosen to serve the smelter at Langley, and the terminus was close to another smelt mill at Catton. The Allenheads extension would include gradients up to 1 in 50, curves of 10 to 12½ch radius, and substantial earthworks. On 19 August 1867 the line opened to goods, minerals and livestock from Hexham to

Langley, and to Catton Road - almost a mile short of Allendale Town - on 13 January 1868. Passenger services, provided by the NER, commenced on 1 March 1869 serving intermediate stations at Elrington, Langley, and Staward.

Hopes for lucrative mineral traffic quickly faded. By 1870 the lead industry was declining, employment in mines and smelters was lost, and the population drifted away. Langley and Allendale smelters closed by the mid-1880s, and only one important lead mine (near Allenheads) survived until World War I. Allendale parish's population fell from 6,401 in 1861 to approximately 2,000 in 1911. In this harsh economic climate, the Allendale Town extension (and the further 7 miles to Allenheads) was not attempted. The struggling Hexham & Allendale was acquired by the NER on 13 July 1876. Although the NER surveyed an extension into Allendale Town in 1898 - the intended terminus if the Allenheads section was abandoned - the railway progressed no further than Catton Road, and that year the terminus was renamed Allendale. Signalling on the branch was unsophisticated. Ground frames, operated by the guard or porter, controlled passing loops at each station and permitted access to sidings.

For a little over 60 years a modest service of passenger trains operated. In 1920 there were three workings each way on weekdays, with an extra afternoon train on Tuesday (Hexham market day) from Hexham to Allendale and back: the service had changed little since the branch opened. Thirty-three minutes were allowed for the Hexham to Allendale journey, and three minutes less for the return. Hexham-based 0-4-4 or 2-4-2 locomotives normally worked the trains. In 1910 a visitor was impressed by the quality of stock, consisting of elliptical-roofed two-bogie carriages, lit by electricity rather than gas. Goods traffic included milk from a creamery near the terminus, lead products, livestock, fodder, timber, coal, and general merchandise. Stone was collected at Glendue Quarry siding, northeast of Elrington. The lonely countryside offered little passenger business, and ticket sales were meagre: Elrington issued only 927 and Langley 2,976 in 1911. Staward's total of 4,547 and Allendale's of 10,691 did not approach half the issues at nearby Fourstones and Haydon Bridge. Ticket sales changed little by 1923, but by 1929 they declined by over 70%; branch station receipts fell by over 80%. In 1926 the economy was made of closing Elrington booking office. In June 1930 the LNER reviewed the finances, and a memorandum to the Traffic, Works, and Locomotive Committees contained the following statistics.

Station	Passengers booked		Receipts £	
	1923	1929	1923	1929
Allendale	11,713	3,493	2,092	358
Staward	3,338	1,173	401	80
Langley	2,860	655	234	51
Elrington	1,155	(Halt)	87	-

The branch's plight was emphasised by comparing receipts of the first quarters of 1929 and 1930: Allendale's fell from £156 to £91; Staward's from £38 to £21; and Langley's from £13 to £9. The losses were unsustainable. Closure would result in an estimated loss of £1,685 revenue (including bookings to the line from Hexham and beyond) but savings in expenditure of £4,687. The breakdown of expenditure was:

Locomotive power	£2,317
Guard	£185
Carriages	£542
Cleaning, lighting, heating, oiling	£184
Station staff	£792
Engineer: permanent way maintenance	£667

One G.5 tank locomotive and 106 coach seats would be released.

After passenger closure it was expected that parcels and 'miscellaneous passenger train traffic' would not suffer appreciable loss of receipts, and that a parcels train would be introduced. The review recognised that buses had caused the branch's financial problems. Robert Emmerson ran buses at two-hourly intervals between Newcastle, Hexham and Allendale Town, via Haydon Bridge. Wharton's buses plied at 75-minute intervals between Hexham, Haydon Bridge, Langley, Catton, and Allendale Town. The fastest buses equalled the train journey time, but linked the centres of Hexham and Allendale, rather than their inconveniently sited stations. Emmerson's was a subsidiary of *United*, an Associated Company of the LNER; the review assumed that a proportion of the rail loss would accrue to that company. It was acknowledged that closure would inconvenience users of Elrington 'where the sparse population will have a little longer walk to the bus than they have at present to join the trains'.

In December 1929, having heard rumours of closure, a deputation from Allendale approached the LNER General Manager to request the retention of the service. They were told that trains were poorly patronised and that, unless traffic increased, no assurance could be given that the service would continue. The review concluded that because of the decline in traffic 'it seems clear that any complaints from the public regarding the withdrawal of the passenger train service can be readily dealt with'. On 22 September 1930 passenger services ended. Goods traffic continued until 20 November 1950. The rails were lifted, and the Ordnance Survey One-inch map published 1956 showed a line remaining only from Elrington to Border Counties Junction. Much of the branch can be traced today. From Glendue to Langley the trackbed is a footpath.

Stations:

Elrington, Langley, Staward, and Allendale opened to passengers on 1 March 1869 and closed on 22 September 1930. They closed entirely on 20 November 1950.

Elrington served a thinly populated hillslope overlooking Haydon Bridge. The least used station on the branch, it issued, on average, only three tickets per day in 1911. It was renamed Elrington Halt in 1926. The single platform was on the up side. The stone-built station house with lean-to extension presented a gable end to the platform and formerly contained the booking office. A passing loop and goods siding were provided. The platform is still in place, and the station house is a private residence.

Langley was a two-platform station serving a small community, Langley Castle, and a lead smelter reached by a siding about 600yd to the northeast. The station house (still occupied) beside the up platform presented a brick gable-end to the platform, and had a rather ungainly, rendered pent-roofed addition extending to three storeys where the ground fell away from the platforms. Passenger facilities were provided on the up platform in a wooden shed with a pitched roof, central sliding door, and flanking windows. The down platform handled goods and parcels. Following many years as a post office, the former passenger shed has a new use. Together with the platforms and trackbed, it has been delightfully transformed by Jane Torday, into *The Garden Station*. Her aim is 'to preserve the sense of a secret garden hidden in the woods'. Gardening courses are held here, and plants are for sale. (From 1936 the station was renamed Langley-on-Tyne.)

Staward was named after neighbouring farms and a derelict tower. Adjacent to the A686 road and the junction of the West and East Allen valleys, it was the railhead for livestock traffic from a wide area. The diminutive goods yard possessed 'coal cells' - storage areas beneath the rails into which coal was poured through hatches opened in the waggons. The stone-built house faced the single up-side platform. Passenger facilities were in a pent-roof wooden shed, with a central door flanked by windows. The house, formerly let as a holiday cottage by British Railways, is well preserved, and the platform is intact. (From 1939 the station was renamed Staward Halt.)

Bishopside Halt between Allendale and Staward appeared in the LNER working timetable (September 1938). The 6.55 pm up goods called for milk traffic.

Allendale was the terminus, although it was designed as a through station. It was at the southern end of Catton village and, until 1898, was named Catton Road. The single platform was on the down side; the original section was of stone, but it was extended in a wooden trestle fashion in 1884. The large, plain house, in uncoursed stone with a pitched slate roof, adjoined the platform. In 1884 a glazed lean-to awning was added. The station possessed a turntable and passing loop, as well as coal cells. A creamery was north of the station, adjacent to the goods yard but without a siding. A private branch served Allen smelt mills. Allendale station house and platform remain within a caravan park.

Staward closed to passengers in 1930 and to goods twenty years later, but in July 1970 the station was remarkably well preserved. *(Alan Young)*

Originally called Catton Road, Allendale was built as a through station in anticipation of the extension of the line to Allendale Town and Allenheads.

(Alan Young Collection)

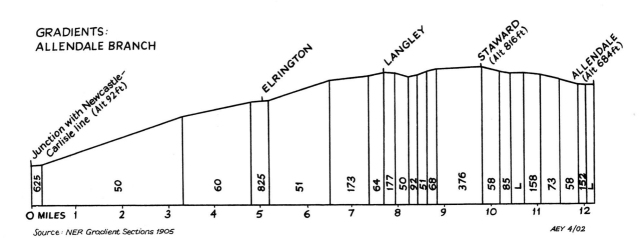

GRADIENTS:
ALLENDALE BRANCH

Source: NER Gradient Sections 1905

AEY 4/02

The Alston Branch

Alston, shortly after diesel multiple units were introduced in 1959. The overall roof, locomotive shed and fitting shop were removed by the mid-1960s.

(J C W Halliday)

Travellers between Newcastle and Carlisle were invited by Haltwhistle's nameboard to 'change for Alston'. From a bay platform overlooking the river, the single-track Alston branch curved alluringly over a viaduct across the South Tyne and disappeared from view, in the direction of the Pennine moorlands and Cumberland. Haltwhistle-Alston was the last surviving passenger branch line in rural North East England. Its longevity reflected the inadequacy of local roads in winter weather, rather than its economic health: 'the creaking gate hangs longest' aptly describes a line that lasted until 1976.

Alston, 1000 ft above sea level, claims to be England's highest market town. Since at least the fifteenth century, lead had been mined, and by 1768, 119 mines operated in Alston parish. Isolation from markets was a handicap. In 1845 rival plans for railways into South Tynedale were deposited before Parliament, promising an end to the lead industry's dependence on packhorse transport. The Wear Valley Extension Railway proposed a route from Frosterley (County Durham) via Stanhope and Alston to Lambley and Milton (Brampton) with a branch from Weardale to Allenheads and Allendale Town. This ambitious scheme required a tunnel under Killhope Moor between the Wear and Tyne river basins. However the Newcastle & Carlisle Railway's proposed Haltwhistle-Alston-Nenthead

branch received the Royal Assent on 26 August 1846. National economic problems delayed construction. When building began, the five-mile section beyond Alston was not proceeded with. The junction at Haltwhistle was adjusted to face Carlisle (the county town of Cumberland, in which Alston was situated) rather than Newcastle. Altogether some 6½ miles of realignments were made to the original route. Additional to the original plans, a branch from Lambley was included to meet the Brampton Railway at Halton Lea Gate. The revised plans received the Royal Assent on 13 July 1849.

The branch required substantial earthworks and structures. There were no watersheds to cross, nor tunnels to bore, but the 13-mile route climbed from 405ft to 905ft above sea level and involved three crossings of the South Tyne and viaducts over tributaries. Most structures were designed for double track and sturdily built of sandstone. The gradient was almost continually uphill from Haltwhistle, including 1 in 70 for 1½ miles between Plenmeller and Featherstone Park; and 1 in 56, the steepest stretch, for a mile near Barhaugh, between Slaggyford and Alston. A mile-long cutting was needed between Haltwhistle and Featherstone Park. Construction began in 1850 from both ends. In March 1851 Haltwhistle-Shaft Hill (Coanwood) opened for goods, and passengers in the following

Featherstone Park c1914. G1 and G2 vans are being shunted over the crossing.

(Dorothy Graham Collection)

July. In January 1852 Alston-Lambley and the Brampton Railway opened, for goods only. Alston-Lambley passenger trains started in May. When Lambley Viaduct was complete, Haltwhistle-Alston services began in November 1852. Intermediate stations were Featherstone, Shaft Hill (closed 1853-62), Lambley, and Slaggyford.

Although N&CR plans to reach Nenthead were abandoned, there were other schemes to extend beyond Alston. An 1864 proposal would have linked Alston with the South Durham & Lancashire Union Railway at Barnard Castle via Yad Moss, Harwood Burn, and Middleton-in-Teesdale. The 1845 idea of reaching Alston from Weardale was revived in 1870; the line's eastern terminus was to be Stanhope (opened in 1862 as an extension to the Frosterley branch). Part of the route eventually materialised, from Stanhope to Wearhead, in 1895.

Any boost that the branch brought to lead mining was short-lived. The industry's decline in the North Pennines began in the 1860s. Depopulation accompanied this economic recession; the population in Alston, Garrigill, and Nenthead peaked at 6,815 in 1851 and fell almost continuously to only 1,909 in 1971. Some cheer was brought by limited development of coal and zinc mining.

In the late 1850s two weekday return passenger trains called at all stations. By 1863 there were three, taking 40 minutes in each direction. The 1910 service increased to four, with an extra Saturday evening return trip, and a five-minute faster journey. Whilst Alston's 'twin' branch to Allendale closed to passengers in 1930, Alston still had its 1910 frequency. In summer 1946 Alston enjoyed eight weekday return trains, the first departure at 5.41 am, but by summer 1954 there were seven on Saturdays and only five on weekdays. Since the early days, the first advertised service of the day left Alston, where the branch locomotive was stabled. This practice continued until November 1959 when a 6.30 am departure from Haltwhistle was introduced, running non-stop (another novelty!) to Alston in thirty minutes, to form the 7.05 am departure (all stops) to Haltwhistle. British Rail censuses in 1970 found no passengers using the first Haltwhistle-Alston train. By its final timetable there were six weekday and seven Saturday returns.

The advertised passenger train service concealed some eccentricities. Plenmeller Halt, near Haltwhistle, was omitted from public timetables. Elsewhere unscheduled stops enabled passengers to join and leave trains. I recall occasions in the 1960s when trains stopped at Park Village and Burnstones (neither with platforms), and at an unidentified point between Lambley and Slaggyford; here a passenger joined the lunchtime train for Alston, leaving her gumboots beside the line. She alighted at the same point in the afternoon, with her shopping, to reoccupy the boots and walk across the fields! With equal informality, if no-one wished to join or alight, trains sometimes coasted through stations without stopping, even when booked to call.

Jenkins (*The Alston Branch*, 1991) assumes that motive power was provided in the mid-19th Century by former main line engines. Towards the end of that century Fletcher BTP 0-4-4Ts (classified as G6 by the LNER) were used, though in the NER period Worsdell Class A 2-4-2 Passenger Tanks were also employed. At first one engine was based at Alston. By 1900 there were two, one for passenger and the other for goods trains. Two elliptical-roof bogie coaches carried passengers in the early 20th Century, with a spare stabled at Alston. In the LNER period G5 0-4-4 and A8 4-6-2 tanks operated the passenger trains. Goods were hauled by J21 and J39 tender engines. The 1950s saw a variety of steam locomotives on the branch including ex-LMS 4MT 2-6-0 and 3MT 2-6-0's. Passenger services were progressively taken over by dmus (generally Metro-Cammell Class 101) from autumn 1959, which operated until closure. However, German 56-seat railbuses were trialled on the branch in 1965. They gave a rough ride and were mechanically unreliable. Consequently they were not adopted, although they worked some East Anglian branches.

Closure - and beyond

The Alston Branch outlived many lines whose passenger carrying potential was greater. Blyth and Ashington, towns of some 30,000 people, lost their service in 1964; Featherstone Park, serving several hundred, survived until 1976. Cost-cutting measures were taken. Featherstone Park and Slaggyford became unstaffed in 1954, and Coanwood in 1955. The first serious threat to the branch was in 1959 when the line was reviewed, but the NE Transport Users' Consultative Committee reported that road services could not adequately replace trains, and closure was rejected. Severe weather in early 1963 disrupted road transport, yet trains continued, providing a 'life-line' for remote communities. Beeching (March 1963) noted that closure of the branch was already under consideration, but on 22 July Ernest Marples, Minister of Transport, announced that the service would continue; this was

Lambley had a fine, Tudor-esque building, and a splendid valley-side setting.
(Martin Bairstow Collection)

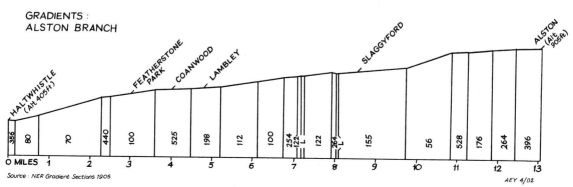

GRADIENTS :
ALSTON BRANCH

Source : NER Gradient Sections 1905

AEY 4/02

the first decision on a proposed line closure following the Beeching Report. The sole criterion for retention of the service was hardship that closure would cause. Further economies were made. Alston's trainshed was dismantled. Lambley and Alston were de-staffed in 1966 and 1969 respectively. Goods services ceased in 1965, and in 1966 the 'one engine in steam' system began, allowing Coanwood, Lambley, and Alston signal boxes to close. Crossing gates and gate boxes at Featherstone Park and Coanwood were removed, trains having to give way to road traffic. Most signals were dismantled, although some fixed distant semaphores were retained, set at caution; one such signal was south of Featherstone Park. At Alston, for some time, a run-round facility remained.

By 1968 the pace of closures had slackened, and a 'basic network' of railways to be retained for passengers and freight in Britain was published; Alston was not included. Under Section 39 of the 1968 Transport Act the branch received a grant of £43,000 for 1969, but the Minister of Transport warned that aid could not be justified for more than two years. In November 1970 BR again proposed closure. Earnings of the line were quoted at £4,000 per annum; the subsidy had risen to £77,000. A one-off expenditure of £300,000 to construct an 'all-weather' road between Coanwood and Lambley was considered prudent use of public money. Censuses of passenger journeys in the weeks ending 22 August

and 24 October 1970, revealed that 60 people regularly used the branch for journeys to work or for shopping trips. The busiest train was the 12.00 on Saturday (24 October) that left Haltwhistle with 40 passengers; many trains carried no more than 10-20 passengers at any stage in their journey, and some ran empty. The document proposing closure identified regular passengers and compared their railway journey to the alternative using existing or proposed road services. Generally the road alternative would take longer, and at Coanwood - the station having the greatest number of known regular passengers - no bus service would be available to former rail users. Objectors to the closure included Northumberland and Cumberland County Councils, Haltwhistle and Alston Rural District Councils, the Northern Rural Development Board, and the Lakes Counties Travel Association. The importance of the service during severe winter weather was stressed, as was the dependence of ramblers and other tourists on trains. Featherstone Park was used by school parties visiting Featherstone Castle. (The party in which I was a pupil in 1967 travelled by hired coach from Newcastle!). Following TUCC deliberations, in January 1973 it was announced that services would be withdrawn, subject to the improved Haltwhistle-Alston road link.

In its last months, British Rail belatedly publicised the Alston branch. The charms of the line were extolled, and trips were recommended by scheduled

The branch goods engine J21 No 5100 pilots a G5 over Lambley Viaduct. The double heading was just a convenient means of returning the goods engine from Haltwhistle to Alston. *(N E Stead Collection)*

G5 0-6-0T No 67241 pulling away from Lambley with a Haltwhistle to Alston train. (*N E Stead Collection*)

services from London. A 'circular' bargain-fare was available from King's Cross and Euston, via Carlisle or Newcastle, to Alston. On the last day of service, Saturday 1 May 1976, some 5,000 passengers travelled on scheduled services on the branch, with yet more on special trains. The final train left Alston at 21.09 to the accompaniment of a lament played by two pipers, and the thunder of detonators. On 3 May 1976 rail services officially ended.

In January 1977 South Tynedale communities were isolated; roads were blocked by snow. This time the railway could not come to the rescue. The South Tynedale Railway Preservation Society was eager to keep the line in operation, but could not afford the purchase price of £160,000 asked by British Rail. Track dismantling began in winter 1976-77. In March 1977 STRPS had the option to buy the last 1½ miles of track, from Gilderdale to Alston, for £40,800. Once again the price proved too high. Demolition continued, and all rails were lifted by June 1977. Happily, this is not the end of the story. Cumbria County Council bought Alston station and the Cumbrian section of trackbed in 1979, enabling the station to serve as a tourist information centre. In 1983 the STRPS opened a 2ft gauge tourist railway at Alston, its trains hauled by *Phoenix,* a forty year-old 4-wheeled Hibberd 40hp diesel locomotive. The line was extended 1½ miles to Gilderdale Halt in 1986; a Light Railway Order was obtained in October 1987 for this section. A further ³/4 mile to Kirkhaugh Halt opened in September

1999, and Gilderdale closed. The South Tynedale Railway intends to reach Slaggyford - having obtained planning permission for this project in 1986 - and ultimately Haltwhistle.

Viaducts

The branch had two splendid stone viaducts designed by Sir George Barclay-Bruce. Both have Grade II status. **Lambley Viaduct** was the highlight of a journey along the branch. It was narrow, built to accommodate only a single track. This, combined with its great height (110ft above the South Tyne), delicate piers, Romanesque arches, and slight curvature, lent particular grace and elegance to the structure. The nine major arches, each of 58ft span, were accompanied by seven further spans of 20ft, and two of 12ft. Southbound passengers not only had an unforgettable vista of the river in its wooded gorge when crossing the viaduct, but were allowed a view back towards the viaduct, as the railway curved sharply through Lambley station. Passengers in the leading dmu car shared the driver's exhilarating view, as the train appeared almost to tiptoe along a tightrope, so narrow was the viaduct. Even the sound was spectacular, the clattering of the train and the screech from its wheel flanges as it left the viaduct echoing across the valley. The other listed viaduct at **Burnstones,** or Thinhope Burn, is modest (37ft high) but is distinguished by having five arches skewed in one direction and one blind arch skewed the other way. Further viaducts survive at Haltwhistle, Slaggyford, Knar Burn, Lintley Burn, Lort Burn, Gilderdale Burn, and Alston.

Stations

Fawcett (2001) is persuaded by available evidence that Benjamin Green, who designed Newcastle & Berwick stations, was also architect of those on the Alston branch. Alston is distinctly N&B in character. Fawcett describes the intermediate station buildings as 'economical but picturesque' symmetrical two-storey houses distinguished by a steeply gabled projecting centre.

Tickets issued at Alston Branch stations

	1911	1951
Featherstone Park	15,094	4,653
Coanwood	7,317	12,469
Lambley	6,976	13,272
Slaggyford	5,940	5,659
Alston	12,349	6,279

Plenmeller Halt was omitted from public timetables. Situated a little over ³/₄ mile from Haltwhistle, it opened in 1919 for Plenmeller Colliery. (Ten years earlier a colliery siding was installed.) The halt had a 33yd earth and sleeper platform on the down side of the running line. In the early 1920s workmen's trains called between 2.00 and 5.00 am, and some public trains stopped in the evening. The colliery closed in 1932, and the halt was abandoned. During World War II a Ministry of Supplies depot opened here, and the halt was revived until 1946. Later, employees of the Cascelloid factory unofficially joined or alighted from trains at Plenmeller, although the platform had been removed.

Featherstone Park was a station of exceptional charm. My first visit was in September 1962. Travelling from Newcastle with a school friend, we alighted at Haltwhistle and walked to Featherstone Park to catch the 12.08 pm for Alston. The station resembled a neglected farmyard. Hens wandered around on the platform's crumbling tarmac. Victorian oil lanterns adorned the platform, with tiny tablets giving the station name; one rendered it 'Featherston Park'. Behind the platform stretched the disused loading dock ending with a grassy bank; here, many yards from the passenger platform, was the large, lopsided nameboard. It was painted in a russet colour, the letters of the station name thinly outlined in black, without any white infill, and almost illegible. At the southern end of the platform were the house and hipped-roofed signal box, adjacent to the level crossing. Beyond the gated level crossing and, like the passenger facilities, west of the running line, was an abandoned signal box. Derelict coal cells faced the old signal box. Shortly before the train arrived, a woman emerged from the house, entered the signal box to open the crossing gates and set the home signal at off. Tickets were no longer sold at Featherstone Park. A conductor-guard collected fares and issued paper tickets from a portable machine. To the disappointment of ticket enthusiasts, these were anonymous 'bus'-type tickets, making no reference to the journey's origin or destination.

The station began life as Featherstone. 'Park' was added in 1902, to avoid confusion with Featherstone (Lancashire & Yorkshire Railway). It served the hamlet of Rowfoot, the Castle (¹/₂ mile west) and a colliery (³/₄ mile southeast). Coal reached the Alston Branch by a tramway, and was loaded into rail waggons in sidings between Featherstone Park and Coanwood. Miners accounted for much of the passenger traffic; in 1911, 15,094 tickets were issued, more than twice the number of any other intermediate station, and almost 3,000 more than at Alston! During World War I the station served a military camp. Afterwards, with mining ended, passenger traffic declined so greatly that the LNER downgraded the station from 1932-40, with 'check-tickets' being issued and the fare paid at the destination. It was renamed Featherstone Park Halt from 1933-37. World War II revived business, with a military camp and prisoners-of-war housed in the domains of Featherstone Castle. In peacetime, passenger traffic declined again. In 1951 only 4,653 tickets were issued: the busiest intermediate station had become the quietest. The solitude made it ideal for parking the royal train overnight when King George VI visited Tyneside. In 1954 goods traffic ceased, and the station became unstaffed. It was not renamed 'Halt'; the North Eastern did not share other BR regions' enthusiasm for the suffix. However it was so named in an Eastern Region handbill of 1967 - along with the other intermediate stations. A sign at the level crossing advised passengers that the station was an Unstaffed Halt, and the implications for ticket purchase. After the branch's reprieve in 1963, Featherstone Park and the other intermediate stations were among the first BR stations to have 'corporate identity' black-and-white nameboards installed, looking incongruous alongside vintage lanterns.

The stone-built house, now a private residence, had two storeys. On the platform elevation, were the main gable-end and a ground floor bay window. The main central section was flanked by a two-storey wing to the south and another of one storey to the north. The 86yd platform was stone fronted with tarmac surface. At its southern end, in front of the house, its height was reduced and it ended vertically, with a wooden ramp added.

Coanwood. A station named Shaft Hill opened here as temporary southern terminus, only to disappear from the timetable from 1853. In 1863 it reopened, as Shafthill, and, in 1885 was renamed Coanwood. It served small mining and quarrying communities. Coanwood Colliery adjoined the railway station, and a limestone quarry was a little south. Both were rail-served and closed by 1920. East Coanwood Colliery, reached by a tramway, closed before World War II. East of the running line was the single 83yd platform, with a 308yd passing

Featherstone Park in September 1962. Note the unusual spelling on the lantern glass and the illegible nameboard on the goods platform.
(Alan Young)

Approaching Lambley station on 19 July 1968.
(Alan Young)

Slaggyford on 9 March 1968.   *(Alan Young)*

On 2 January 1973 a class 101 dmu stands at Alston.
(Alan Young)

loop to its west. Immediately south was a level crossing. Beyond, on the down side, was a small goods yard. The permanent passenger station was built in 1877-78. To the north of the platform, set well back at right angles, was the two-storey house. Waiting and booking facilities were in a pitched-roofed wooden shed. The central portion was recessed to provide an open-fronted shelter. Adjacent to the south was a wooden hut, adopted as the shelter when the main buildings were demolished, probably in the early 1960s. An 1890s plan shows a signal box on the platform north of the passenger buildings. This was replaced some ten years later with a typical NER box, as at Featherstone Park. Coanwood issued 7,317 tickets in 1911, rising to 12,469 in 1951. Nevertheless, in 1955, BR closed the booking office, de-staffed the station, and withdrew the goods service. Having lost its nameboard and lantern nameplates by 1963, Coanwood acquired a large BR corporate identity nameboard. After closure the platform and trackbed reverted to nature.

Lambley was magnificently sited, with a fine view of the viaduct. Passengers reached the station by a 500yd rough track. The house, located where the original low platform met the later platform's northern ramp, was Tudoresque with a prominent central gable. The toilet and waiting facilities were added in the 1890s in a single-storey wooden southward extension. A two-storey domestic block stood at the other side. The Brampton Railway branched off immediately north of the station, leading to Lambley Colliery. Because of the cramped site there was no passing loop at the 100yd platform, but goods trains could shunt back onto the colliery line. The station was staffed until 1966. After closure the house remained in residential use.

Whitwham, Softley, and **Burnstones** were unofficial stopping places between Lambley and Slaggyford.

Slaggyford station stood immediately north of a level crossing. On the single 90yd-platform west of the running line, a timber shed (constructed in 1890) housed the booking office and two waiting rooms. A brick-built NER signal box was on the same side of the tracks. The stationmaster's house, closely resembling that at Lambley, stood east of the rails close to the goods store. A 242yd passing loop was installed. The platform and shed remain in good repair and the trackbed is passable; the station house is in residential use.

Alston's layout comprised a single 106yd passenger platform east of the running line, a carriage siding to the west, and several sidings either side of the platform. The southern end of the platform had steps, rather than a ramp. The turntable at the terminus was disused by 1951. The station building was an imposing structure of Newcastle & Berwick type, with random stone courses instead of the more urbane ashlar. Unfortunately, rendering of three sides marred its appearance. In 1904-5 a single-storey extension was added. A trainshed was supported by the station building, and covered the platform and two tracks. Its west side was joined to the engine shed, a smith's shop, and a water tower. The curved roof was extended and rebuilt with a mansard profile in the 1870s. It was dismantled in the mid-1960s. Goods installations included a three-ton crane and facilities for handling livestock, furniture, coal, lime, and ore. Goods services ceased in 1965 and the station was de-staffed in 1969. Although removal of the trainshed and sidings left the station somewhat bleak, it retained delightful fixtures at closure: the LNER nameboard, gas lamps, and a North Eastern Railway enamel 'Way Out' sign. After closure the site, stripped of its tracks, was forlorn, but restoration of the building and the introduction of narrow-gauge trains have revitalised Alston station.

A Metro Cammell dmu at Alston on 30 December 1961. The snow helped to keep the line open until an all weather road was completed fifteen years later.

(Geoffrey C Lewthwaite)

The Brampton Railway

The Brampton Town branch was abandoned as early as 1923. A Class BTP 0-4-4T is seen here at Brampton Town.
(N E Stead Collection)

The Earl of Carlisle owned collieries on the Tindale Fells east of Brampton. Wooden waggonways served these mines by the late-18th Century. On 15 April 1799 a route of about 5 miles opened from Tarnhouse Colliery to Brampton, part of which was re-laid with iron rails within ten years. It was gradually extended to collieries at Midgeholme, Halton Lea Gate, and Lambley using 4ft 8½ in gauge; the rest of the route was ultimately altered to this gauge. The Brampton Railway's offices and engineering works were at Kirkhouse (between Milton and Hallbankgate). By 1835 passengers were carried on the Brampton Railway from Midgeholme to Brampton market, in four-wheel horse-drawn coaches named *Black Diamond, Experiment,* and *Mountaineer.*

When the Newcastle & Carlisle Railway route was established, the Brampton Railway's course was adjusted to meet the N&CR at Milton (later renamed Brampton Junction). The realigned route opened on 13 July 1836, six days before the N&CR. From this date, passengers informally joined and alighted from trains at Kirkhouse. The illustrious locomotive *Rocket,* rejected by the Liverpool & Manchester Railway, was bought by the Earl of Carlisle. In a modified form it operated on the Midgeholme section. Soon after the line's official opening, a horse-drawn 'dandy' passenger service began on the 1¼ miles between Milton and Brampton, whilst coal trains were steam-hauled. This arrangement persisted until 1 July 1881 when the Brampton Railway introduced a steam-hauled passenger service, using *Dandie Dinmont,* an 0-6-0 side tank, and three ex-LNWR four-wheeled carriages. A single-platform station was provided east of the track, known as Brampton Town. However the service was short-lived. The management were reluctant to pay for

improvements to bring the line up to Board of Trade safety standards, so passenger trains ceased on 30 April 1890. Changes to the leaseholding of the collieries and railway proved obstructive to Brampton residents' demands for the restoration of their passenger trains. Eventually the NER agreed a 50-year lease, with the dowager Countess of Carlisle, on the railway and coal deposits at Brampton. They re-laid the single track and made other improvements, which included an adequate booking office, waiting room, and engine run-round loop at Brampton Town. The branch reopened to passengers on 1 August 1913. A 'steam autocar' consisting of a BTP locomotive coupled to a coach at each end, shuttled to-and-fro, connecting with Newcastle/Carlisle trains. In 1914 over 14,000 passengers were carried. However the service ceased again, on 1 March 1917, as a wartime economy measure. On 1 March 1920 services resumed, but passenger traffic failed to reach expectations, and heavy losses were incurred. The NER decided to discontinue leasing the coal deposits from October 1923, and the lessor expressed no interest in taking responsibility for the railway. So on 29 October 1923 passenger services were finally withdrawn by the LNER (successor to the NER) and goods services ended on 31 December. The tracks were lifted in 1924. Part of the branch is now a footpath.

The Brampton Junction-Lambley line developed several branches serving small collieries, quarries, and a spelter works. 1½ miles of track between Midgeholme and Lambley Colliery closed in 1908, though the tracks were not lifted for some years. Midgeholme-Brampton Junction closed in 1953. The remaining Lambley Colliery-Lambley Station section closed on 2 May 1960. Much of the route is well preserved.

The North British Railway Lines

Reedsmouth in summer 1955. Class J21 0-6-0 No 65110 with a Newcastle-Rothbury Gardens Excursion via Hexham, Bellingham, and Scotsgap, returning via Morpeth
(K H Cockerill / J W Armstrong Trust Collection)

From the mid-1870s the North Eastern Railway operated most of northeast England's passenger railways. However a quarter of Northumberland passenger routes belonged to the North British Railway, a Scottish company based in Edinburgh. In 1923 the NER and NBR were brought together within the LNER, yet the NBR system in Northumberland retained its character. The 74 miles of single-track railways served remote, beautiful and tranquil countryside; but they grew out of intense rivalry between the Scottish company, determined to reach Newcastle and share in the wealth of the Northumbrian coalfield, and the NER, equally determined to keep them out. After inter-company rivalry subsided in the mid-1880s, a few trains made leisurely journeys daily serving remote communities in the North Tyne and Wansbeck valleys. Small mines and quarries provided traffic, and farmers looked to the railway to transport livestock. Although the NBR system was hardly profitable it provided a lifeline for an isolated area. The railway staff understood the needs of the communities they served; for example newspapers were dropped off at line-side cottages, and the guard conveyed medicine from doctor to patient.

Stationmasters found time to tend gardens, and special trains ran to allow passengers to admire their handiwork. Rothbury branch trains sometimes stopped for passengers and train crew to pick blackberries or catch rabbits! Harsh economic reality destroyed this way of life, and the system closed to passengers between 1952 and 1956. No longer would six men - two drivers, two firemen and two guards - be employed to move one railway carriage 59 miles a day (Scotsgap-Reedsmouth/Bellingham), or Knowesgate station survive on issuing fewer than five tickets a week.

The Border Counties Railway

This 42-mile, single-track railway began at Border Counties Junction, west of Hexham. It followed the North Tyne to its source at Deadwater, the scenery changing from lush pastures to moorland beyond Bellingham. Entering Scotland at Deadwater the line continued several miles to meet the 'Waverley Route' at Riccarton Junction. The region was very thinly populated: Bellingham (1,200 inhabitants) was the largest place served. From the 1920s much of the moorland was transformed by the planting of Kielder Forest.

The North Tyne valley was identified, but rejected, as a possible Anglo-Scottish railway route by a Commission of 1839. In 1846 the Newcastle & Carlisle unsuccessfully proposed a Hexham-Bellingham-Woodburn branch to join the projected Newcastle, Edinburgh & Direct Glasgow Railway. However on 31 July 1854 the Border Counties Railway, chaired by local landowner, W. H. Charlton, obtained consent for a Hexham-Bellingham-The Belling (near Falstone) line. The project engineer was J.F.Tone, and William Hutchinson was contractor. On 11 August 1859 - by which time the BCR had opened from Hexham to Chollerford - an extension into Scotland was approved, to meet the North British Border Union Railway at Riccarton. This Hawick-Carlisle line, part of the Edinburgh-Carlisle 'Waverley Route', had itself been approved on 21 July 1859. The North British, determined to reach Tyneside, was

prepared to help finance the Border Counties extension and operate the line. As part of this strategy the NBR Chairman was a board member of the Wansbeck Valley Railway, which obtained approval on 8 August 1859 for a 25¼-mile railway from the Border Counties near Bellingham to Morpeth, linking with the Blyth & Tyne Railway. This would allow NBR working between Scotland and New Bridge Street, Newcastle (opened 1864) without using NER metals. Access to Blyth's port would also be obtained. However full running powers between Hexham and Newcastle were gained by the North British when the NER absorbed the N&C in 1863. The independent NBR route via Bellingham and Morpeth became unnecessary, and the planned junction with the Wansbeck Valley route, originally intended to be at Bellingham, was changed to Reedsmouth instead, and faced Hexham.

Chollerton. This platform with its simple shed was constructed by the North British Railway immediately north west of the original Border Counties Railway station.
(J F Sedgwick / N E Stead Collection)

Barrasford is one of many ex-NBR stations in Northumberland to remain intact long after closure. Seen here in August 2001 the building is used a scout hostel. *(Alan Young)*

Enough land along the Border Counties line was bought for double track, and major masonry structures (except Border Counties Bridge) were built to double track dimensions and were of excellent quality. However a single track sufficed. The line rose from about 120ft at Hexham to about 870ft approaching Riccarton, with a ruling gradient of 1 in 100. The difficult terrain required numerous curves and earthworks, and several viaducts. Border Counties Bridge, immediately north of Border Counties Junction, and east of the confluence of the rivers North and South Tyne, had four spans over the river and smaller spans on the north bank. The wrought-iron girders were carried 15ft above water level on cast-iron tubular piers. This bridge was subject to severe erosion, partly offset by cutwaters. Following the August 1948 floods, the southern span needed strengthening with timber props. After closure the piers and girders were removed. At Reedsmouth the five skew-arch Rede Bridge was of stone and 30ft high. Only the piers survive today. Kielder Viaduct was the line's finest structure, 130yd long and 55ft high, and decorated with battlements to complement Kielder Castle. The sophisticated design of skew-arches used a system devised by Peter Nicholson, a Newcastle geometrician, whereby each stone was individually shaped. The viaduct is designated an Ancient Monument. A five-span viaduct - now demolished - crossed Dawstonburn, near Saughtree. Smaller skew-arch viaducts survive at Chollerford and Tarset.

The first section, Hexham to Chollerford, opened to passengers on 5 April 1858. Four weekday and two Sunday trains ran each way. On 1 December 1859 the line was extended to Countess Park, about 1 3/4 miles south of Reedsmouth. *Bradshaw* of December 1860 showed three Hexham-Countess Park weekday trains each way, the two return Sunday trains working only to Wark. In February 1861 Countess Park closed when the line was extended to Thorneyburn. The section to Falstone opened in September 1861. Riccarton was reached in April 1862 (before the Border Union line was finished), goods services being introduced in June, and passenger trains in July 1862.

In 1863 the Border Counties had four weekday and two Sunday trains in each direction taking approximately two hours for the 42-mile trip. By 1870 the service was reduced to three weekday trains. Even in 1863 certain trains omitted some station calls; in 1870 Saughtree and Thorneyburn had fewest trains. Thorneyburn had only one request stop in each direction on Saturdays and was relegated to the footnotes. By 1910 the three weekday trains were supplemented by a Saturday train at 2.15 pm (Bellingham-Hexham) and a 7.00 pm (Hexham-Bellingham). A mid-afternoon return service from the Wansbeck Valley worked between Bellingham and Reedsmouth. Now Thorneyburn enjoyed only a Tuesday service with a southbound departure at 7.24 am and northbound at 12.50 pm allowing a visit to Hexham market. The 1943 timetable still showed three weekday trains -with a daily service each way calling at Thorneyburn- but no extra Saturday workings.

The final summer timetable (NE Region 1956) is reproduced. Wall station (closed 1955) is absent. The extra Saturday trains principally served Forestry Commission workers and families at Kielder. The regular Saturday night train from Hexham replaced an unusual arrangement that lasted from 1948 until 1952 whereby, on alternate Saturdays, late night trains ran (1952 timings) from Hexham (dep 10.30 pm) to Kielder Forest (arr 11.54 pm) and from Hawick (dep 10.57 pm) to Falstone (arr 12.7 on Sunday morning). Residents of remote communities at Falstone, Plashetts, Lewiefield, and Kielder could therefore 'live-it-up' alternately in the closest English and Scottish towns. Deadwater residents were permitted only a fortnightly Scottish Saturday night in Hawick; how many revellers alighted from the return train at a quarter to midnight on Deadwater's platform amid the empty moorlands?

Motive power was at first 2-2-2 and 2-4-0 tender engines, giving way to 4-4-0's and 0-6-0's working passenger and freight respectively. In LNER days some ex-NER locomotives were allocated. A variety of engines was used, including 0-6-0, 2-6-0, 4-4-0, and 4-6-0. In the final years V1 and V3 tank engines and BR standard 76000 and 77000 series operated the line. Early rolling stock was of four-wheel and later six-wheel type. In later NBR days bogie coaches were adopted. The LNER used ex-NER clerestory coaches. After World War II corridor coaches were belatedly introduced - Gresley, Thompson, and BR Mark I. Whilst three coaches were regularly used at first, by the 1950s one coach often sufficed. Dmus appeared latterly on special trains, including ramblers' excursions.

Goods traffic on the Border Counties included livestock - there were marts at Hexham, Bellingham, and Scotsgap- coal and coke, stone, lime, road chippings, cement, pipes, timber, and beer. In the 1930s the railway conveyed the seedlings for Kielder Forest. In World War II military supplies were carried to training areas. Sidings along the route served industrial premises. Acomb Colliery, east of the line, between Hexham and Wall had a branch by 1870 and operated until 1952. A little to the north was North Tyne Colliery, with a branch and loop; this pit closed in 1922. Tramways extended into Cocklaw (south of Chollerton) and Barrasford quarries, and sidings handled their traffic. At Gunnerton a public siding was used from about 1890 to 1920 by a sawmill. Mill Knock siding near Countess Park served a quarry tramway at the time of World War I. In the early days a siding served a colliery and tileworks west of Thorneyburn. Hawkhope Hill drift mine, north of Falstone, had a siding and tramway. In the 1860s-70s sidings served Bellsburn Quarry, one mile north of Kielder; Thorlieshope limeworks, northwest of Deadwater; and Muirdykes Quarry a further half-mile beyond. In addition mineral branches joined at Humshaugh and Plashetts stations.

Closure

Passenger bookings for 1951 indicate the limited traffic of this rural railway. The five stations in the lower valley issued few tickets, despite being in the more densely populated part of the valley. They were badly sited for the villages they served, and for over twenty years buses had operated between Hexham and Bellingham, passing through the villages and offering a more frequent, cheaper service. In 1931 Moffit's ran six buses each way on this route on Monday-Friday, twice as many on Saturday between Humshaugh and Hexham, and several Sunday journeys. The Hexham-Bellingham journey was 50 minutes - almost the same as by train. The upper valley lacked regular buses. Although Plashetts' population had largely drifted away by 1951, there was no road access and the few inhabitants, of necessity, used the train. Deadwater's traffic was substantially less than its English neighbours, but it served a particularly desolate area.

Station	Tickets issued 1951	Station	Tickets issued 1951
Wall	138	Bellingham	6,589
Humshaugh	478	Tarset	1,616
Chollerton	331	Falstone	2,306
Barrasford	732	Plashetts	2,493
Wark	504	Lewiefield Halt	3,407
Reedsmouth	4,179	Kielder Forest	2,335
		Deadwater	285

No data for Thorneyburn and Saughtree.

Goods traffic also declined after World War II. After 1945 one through goods service used the line. The only local goods train left Riccarton at 7.20 am making an unhurried journey to Hexham and back, collecting and delivering whatever traffic was offered, and following no strict timetable. Reedsmouth shed closed on 13 September 1952. As traffic dwindled, track maintenance was neglected, and by 1955 a general speed limit of 35 mph applied, but only 10 mph over Border Counties Bridge, where a weight restriction was also imposed. After flood damage in 1948 proper repair was not considered worthwhile, and the poor condition of this bridge strengthened the case for closure. Wall closed in 1955, and the entire line closed to passengers on 15 October 1956. The final day of services was Saturday 13 October, when the 11.10 am Newcastle-Hawick, and its return working, were designated a 'closure excursion'. The day's final train was the Saturday-only 9.15 pm Hexham-Kielder Forest in which passengers could return to Hexham (arriving 12.30 am) in what was normally empty stock. (A record of the last day's trains was made on cine film, and was compiled by the BBC into a fascinating programme, *Slow Train to Riccarton Junction*.) Existing bus services were available between Hexham and Bellingham. Beyond Bellingham, no operator was

willing to serve the scattered communities. However the British Transport Commission persuaded Norman Fox Motors to run a replacement service with a subsidy for three years. Thus a service, using elderly *United* vehicles, was introduced between Bellingham and Kielder, extended to Deadwater and Steele Road station (Waverley Line) on Saturdays. Sadly, the TUCC file of correspondence regarding local dissatisfaction with the replacement buses is a weighty one! Hexham-Riccarton goods services continued, and passenger trains occasionally visited the line, the last being a ramblers' excursion on 7 September 1958: goods traffic officially ceased several days earlier, on 1 September. Bellingham-Reedsmouth was retained for one goods train per week, reached via the Wansbeck line, and supervised by Woodburn's stationmaster. Rails north of Bellingham and south of Reedsmouth were removed during 1959, and Border Counties Bridge was demolished, leaving the cutwaters and bases of the piers. The final Border Counties section closed entirely on 11 November 1963, together with Reedsmouth-Woodburn. Two days earlier, a farewell dmu tour visited Bellingham, as well as Rothbury, which closed to all traffic at the same time. In 1964 Bellingham-Reedsmouth rails were lifted.

The Border Counties offers much of interest to the railway archaeologist. Most stations, bridges, cuttings and embankments are intact, and minor structures can be seen, such as a platelayer's hut near Tarset. However, in the late 1970s, seven miles of valley between Kielder and Falstone were flooded to create Kielder Water reservoir, and Plashetts station site is now submerged. (An ambitious plan - the *South Borders Railway* - to reinstate the railway from Kielder to Riccarton and Carlisle, to carry timber from the forest, has been proposed by a company called Border Transport Futures.)

Stations

No single building style was used on the Border Counties, but most structures were of sandstone, sturdy and unassuming. Single passenger platforms were the norm, originally about 50yd long, but in about 1890 the NBR lengthened most of them. At the same time some buildings were altered, and signal boxes of a hipped roof design were installed at certain stations. Reedsmouth alone had two platforms, and a further platform for Wansbeck trains. Stations were originally oil-lit, but electric lighting was later installed, using horizontal beams mounted on straight posts, at Chollerton, Barrasford, Reedsmouth, and Bellingham, also at Riccarton Junction, where hooped posts were used. In BR days most nameboards retained a black background and white raised lettering; however at Humshaugh, Reedsmouth (and possibly Chollerton and Barrasford) boards were repainted in tangerine.

Wall station was half-a-mile south of Wall village. The platform was on the up side, with the single-storey main building adjacent to the south ramp. A short verandah was provided between this and another neat, small stone building, aligned at right angles to the first, and distinguished by enormous windows. These buildings probably date from 1890, when the signal box was installed on the platform. For many years a loop was on the down side opposite the platform. In the 1940s the main building was damaged by fire and not repaired. Thereafter a wooden structure was supplied for passenger shelter. In 1951, the 138 tickets issued at Wall was the lowest figure in Northumberland, and both passenger and goods services ended in 1955. In 1974 the platform survived with the signal box and the more northerly building. Subsequently a cottage, easily mistaken for a station building, has been constructed at the site.

Humshaugh station was delightfully situated close to Chollerford Bridge, the focus of the local roads, where the Military Road crosses the North Tyne. In 1919, to avoid confusion with Chollerton, it was renamed Humshaugh after a village ³/4-mile north. The platform, on the down side, had a substantial and attractive 2-storey house, L-plan with raised gables. A finial embellished the front gable; the chimney on the back gable has, since closure, been removed and replaced with a matching finial. The goods shed had an awning over the passenger platform. This arrangement arose when the platform was extended southwest. There was a passing loop, also sidings, which gave access to a lime depot. Beyond was a narrow-gauge tramway from Brunton Quarry and kilns. For some time a camping coach was installed, surviving in a derelict state after closure. The station was well kept, and in later years had a lawn on the site of the loop. The passenger and goods buildings remain, the house slightly extended, and the trackbed is grassed as part of an attractive garden. Sadly cypresses obstruct the view of the station from the overbridge.

Chollerton station served a nearby hamlet. Originally the short platform on the up side had a twin-pavilion single-storey building with central enclosed verandah, accompanied by semidetached cottages to the north and goods loops and a coal depot to the south. Rather than extend the platform the NBR constructed a new one to the north, with a wooden shelter. The original buildings remained in use. The sidings were reorganised enabling one of the two goods docks to use the old platform. The original buildings survive in residential use. The platform is extant, complete with waiting shelter and lamp posts.

Barrasford station was on the outskirts of the village. Its platform was on the down side, with a timber southeast extension. The pleasant two-storey building presented a gable and ground-floor bay to the platform, flanked by single-storey sections with sloping roofs; the southeast section was added later. The window and door openings had pointed arches. A siding adjoined the running line opposite the platform, and there was a further loop to the northwest. Externally, the building has changed little, and is a scout hostel. Part of the platform is in place.

Wark is an attractive village west of the River North Tyne. The station was situated a mile east. The platform was on the down side. Wark's station building resembled Barrasford, but had raised gables. The remainder of the building, at right-angles, was also two-storey, with arched windows downstairs facing the platform. The layout of sidings changed during the station's life. By 1900 it included a loop opposite the platform serving a goods dock, and a further siding and goods dock ending at the northwest ramp of the passenger platform. The platform and goods docks survive, and the house is in residential use.

Countess Park, the terminus from 1859-61, possessed a run-round loop and temporary platform. Nothing remains of the station.

Reedsmouth was the local spelling when the BCR/NBR opened the station, and they retained this rendering of the name, rather than Redesmouth. Although popularly called Reedsmouth Junction, nameboards and timetables did not use the suffix. In 1860 there were few dwellings nearby, but the NBR created a village, including a row of cottages on the station approach, later joined by a mission hall and a shop. Reedsmouth's importance depended upon its junction where passengers interchanged between Border Counties and Wansbeck trains, and goods marshalling was carried out. Scottish and English train crews exchanged here, and an engine shed operated until 1952.

At first the station was diminutive, with two staggered platforms and a passing loop. When the planned junction with the Wansbeck Valley Railway was altered to face south, the first station was abandoned, and a new one was built about 100yd south, at the junction. Two platforms served the Border Counties line. A single Wansbeck line platform splayed from the up BCR platform. Two prominent buildings occupied the shared BCR/WVR platform area. A fine, hipped-roof signal box occupied the southern end. Placed at right-angles to the tracks it had a commanding view towards Hexham. To its north was the station building, a robust structure with rounded openings, surmounted by a water tank. The down BCR platform had a hipped-roof waiting shed. An existing underpass was adopted as the subway between the BCR platforms; the LNER replaced this with a footbridge. Adjacent to the WVR running-line were four through sidings, whilst further sidings north of the BCR platforms served the coal depot and engine shed. After closure the station was derelict for many years. Eventually the station building (minus tank) and the signal box were converted for residential use. The former engine shed is also extant.

Bellingham was planned as the junction for the Wansbeck Railway. The platform on the down side was originally 100yd, later extended to 160yd. The smart station building on an embankment had three storeys at the roadside and two on the platform. In this L-plan structure, the southeast section possessed one large, gabled

Tarset on 13 October 1956, the final day of regular passenger trains. Class V3 No 67639, complete with wreath, is on the Kielder Forest-Hexham working.

(J W Armstrong Trust)

Thorneyburn, with its short platform, limited passenger accommodation, and fine North British Railway signal post.

(E E Smith / N E Stead Collection)

Falstone, looking towards Hexham on 15 September 1956, one month before closure.

(Geoffrey C Lewthwaite)

dormer on the platform and road elevations, with arched windows. Its northwest end gables faced the platform and road, and both elevations had paired arched windows on the top storey and a single arch on the storey below. A signal box and a wooden store completed the platform buildings. Sidings were installed northeast of the running line. In 1926 the LNER added the suffix 'North Tyne' to avoid confusion with Bellingham (Southern Railway). Today the station house is well maintained as county council offices. Immediately northwest, a heritage centre stands on part of the old trackbed. The remainder of the site is a car park.

Charlton opened with the line to serve a farming hamlet. It possessed a small, timber platform and shelter, with a siding 200yd east. The station lasted under two years, the siding a little longer. Nothing remains of the station.

Tarset is where the railway leaves the arable and rich grazing land and intermittent woodlands and enters wilder country. The station took its name from a ruined castle nearby. The platform was on the down side accompanied by a siding and goods dock to the southeast. After extension in 1888 -the date is above the exterior door - the single-storey building was L-shape. The station doubled as a Post Office, as did Plashetts and Kielder. The austere building, well suited to its setting, is in residential use.

Thorneyburn, an isolated station on a gated lane, was for seven months the terminus, temporarily equipped with a loop and siding. Its 50yd platform, with a small wooden hut, was never extended. Parcels and goods were not handled. The platform was on the down side, east of a level crossing. A gatekeeper's cottage, doubling as station house, was diagonally opposite beyond the crossing. By 1974 the platform had gone. The railway crossing-gates remained, but were later replaced. The cottage is still occupied.

Falstone was another temporary terminus, in 1861-62. The platform on the up side, extended to 85yd, had a two-storey L-plan house with corbelled gables. A single-storey section extended south. A siding, with goods dock, was set into the south end of the platform, and a loop faced the platform. The site is now owned by the Forestry Commission. The platform and building survive; the building, with some alterations, is in residential and office use.

Plashetts. The BCR hoped to exploit the isolated Plashetts coalfield in the moors northeast of the North Tyne. A station without road access was built at the closest point to it, with railway staff houses, a church hall, and a public house. A brickworks and coke ovens were close to the station. A drift mine was established two miles east, reached by a steeply inclined waggonway. At the incline top, the coal company created a community with some ninety cottages, a school, shop, and chapel, with several houses closer to the mine. For many years the mine prospered, producing domestic coal for the Scottish border towns. However it closed in the General Strike (1926). Underground conditions deteriorated,

nevertheless it briefly reopened with a much-reduced workforce. The colliery villages were abandoned, and in 1952 the Forestry Commission demolished them.

The down side platform had a distinctive single-storey building with round-headed windows, adjoining a water tower, prominently mounted on a two-storey structure. A network of sidings adjacent to the running-line also served installations at the foot of Plashetts Colliery incline. By BR days goods traffic was minimal, and most of the sidings and the signal box had gone. Passenger traffic dwindled too, and from 2 January 1956 the station was unstaffed. In 1974 the platform and building (minus water tower) remained but they were soon demolished, and were flooded by Kielder Water.

Lewiefield Halt. To retrain long-term unemployed people, the government established camps where skills such as land drainage and road building were taught. One known as Lewiefield (later as Kielder) was near the railway on Forestry Commission land. In 1933 the Halt opened to serve it. The timber-faced platform, on the down side, had two small wooden buildings containing a booking office and a waiting room. Oil lamps and a standard LNER nameboard were installed. Enough passenger traffic, civilian and military, was generated to justify staffing the Halt, from 1 June 1938 until 19 September 1955. After closure, the platform survived until the mid-1970s.

Kielder originally served a small community, but between the wars the Forestry Commission added a number of houses for its employees. The platform was on the up side. The station building comprised two semidetached cottages with raised gables, each with a large dormer. A signal box was added later, and a rearrangement of sidings reduced the platform from 85 to 75yd. In early years the platform was served by a loop off the running-line. The station was renamed Kielder Forest in 1948. Today the station buildings are in residential use.

Deadwater. 'In a wild hollow under the English slope [of Peel Fell] the North Tyne springs from peat mosses, and on its way down lingers silently for a time in a rushy flat known to the borderers as Deadwater, a name now embalmed in the timetables of the North British Railway'. So wrote Bradley in *The Romance of Northumberland* (1908). He refers to the 'Liliputian station with a narrow platform' and an outlook that is 'wild, solitary and beautiful, incidentally disclosing a couple of farmhouses and perhaps twice as many cottages'. By 1877, a few yards from Scotland, a timber platform - called Deadwater Foot Crossing - stood on the up side, close to a siding, to serve quarry workers. In 1880 Deadwater became a public station, with a lengthened platform and an austere single-storey building with an extension set back at the northwest end. There was negligible passenger traffic, but the station survived until the line closed, albeit unstaffed from 19 September

Kielder Forest at 1.35 pm on 13 October 1956. Class 3MT No 77011 has the 11.10 am Newcastle to Hawick working. Class V3 No 67867, in the siding, will take the 1.40 pm Saturdays-only train to Hexham.

(J W Armstrong Trust)

1955. An eccentricity of later timetables required passengers wishing to join the 6.55 am southbound train to contact the stationmaster at Riccarton before 5.00 pm the previous day. One wonders how many such requests he received, and why this procedure was in place, rather than timetabling the train to stop! The station is intact, with minor external alterations.

Saughtree was another lonely station. On a bleak hillside, it served a hamlet a mile distant. The down side platform had two adjoining single-storey buildings, the station house with a roof markedly taller than the office and waiting-room building. There was a siding north of the running line. As a wartime economy measure, in 1944 passenger trains ceased to call, but were restored in 1948 with a service limiting passengers to travel within Scotland: a surprising fact since the Scottish and North Eastern 1955 passenger timetable maps placed the station in the NE Region. Trains called on Monday, Thursday and Saturday only; a northbound service at 1.48 pm to uplift passengers, and at 5.08 pm southbound (5.10 pm on Saturday) to set them down. This allowed shoppers two hours in Hawick, three days per week including Thursday, the market day. (The Scottish Region timetable confined Saughtree to a footnote.) The station has undergone restoration and a short stretch of railway track has been installed.

Riccarton Junction. The Border Union (Waverley) line met the Border Counties at a remote inaccessible site in the hills, where the only habitation was a shepherd's cottage. The railway adopted the name Riccarton from a tower and farm some distance south and a burn that rose nearby. A village of 37 houses was built for railway workers and their families, together with a school and mission hall. The station buildings contained a branch of Hawick Co-op and a Post Office. Church services were held in the waiting room, the minister

reaching the station by walking along the railway from Saughtree. Burials were not conducted at Riccarton: coffins were conveyed to Newcastleton, where interment took place. The station at Riccarton ('Junction' from 1905) was located amidst a maze of sidings that served an engine shed, carriage shed, goods warehouse, coal depot, smithy, and gas plant. The 280yd island platform had bays at each end, the southern one for Border Counties trains. The north bay was abandoned and infilled before closure. A footbridge gave access to the village, which overlooked the station from the northeast. Signal boxes stood at each end of the station. The range of single-storey platform buildings lacked architectural merit.

The isolated community thrived until the 1960s, entirely dependent on the railways for access. Electricity reached Riccarton in 1955: amidst great excitement, cookers and other electrical gadgets were hauled to the village from the station by sledge. Although Border Counties trains ceased in 1958 the Waverley route survived until 6 January 1969. Riccarton's goods services had already been withdrawn on 6 Feburary 1967, and from that date it became an unstaffed halt. For some years before and after closure there were attempts by the Border Union Railway Preservation Society to keep the Waverley line alive as a private enterprise, but their efforts were fruitless and the tracks were lifted.

I visited Riccarton in January 1978, driving there along several miles of rutted tracks. In a wasteland formerly occupied by sidings the platforms, buildings, footbridge, southern signal box complete with lever-frame, and even a phone box remained. The railway cottages had gone. Only the school-house was still occupied, attended by a vociferous dog whose incessant barking was the only sound to be heard. The stationmaster's house was also present, but derelict. Five years later, much of the station had been demolished.

Riccarton Junction, looking south on 6 October 1956. The buildings on the island platform included a refreshment room run by the local co-operative society.

(J C W Halliday)

Deadwater on 20 September 1952. This isolated Northumbrian station stood a few yards from the Scottish border.
(J W Armstrong Trust)

K1 2-6-0 No 62006 at Riccarton Junction with the 4.32 pm Hawick to Newcastle on Saturday 6 October 1956.
(J C W Halliday)

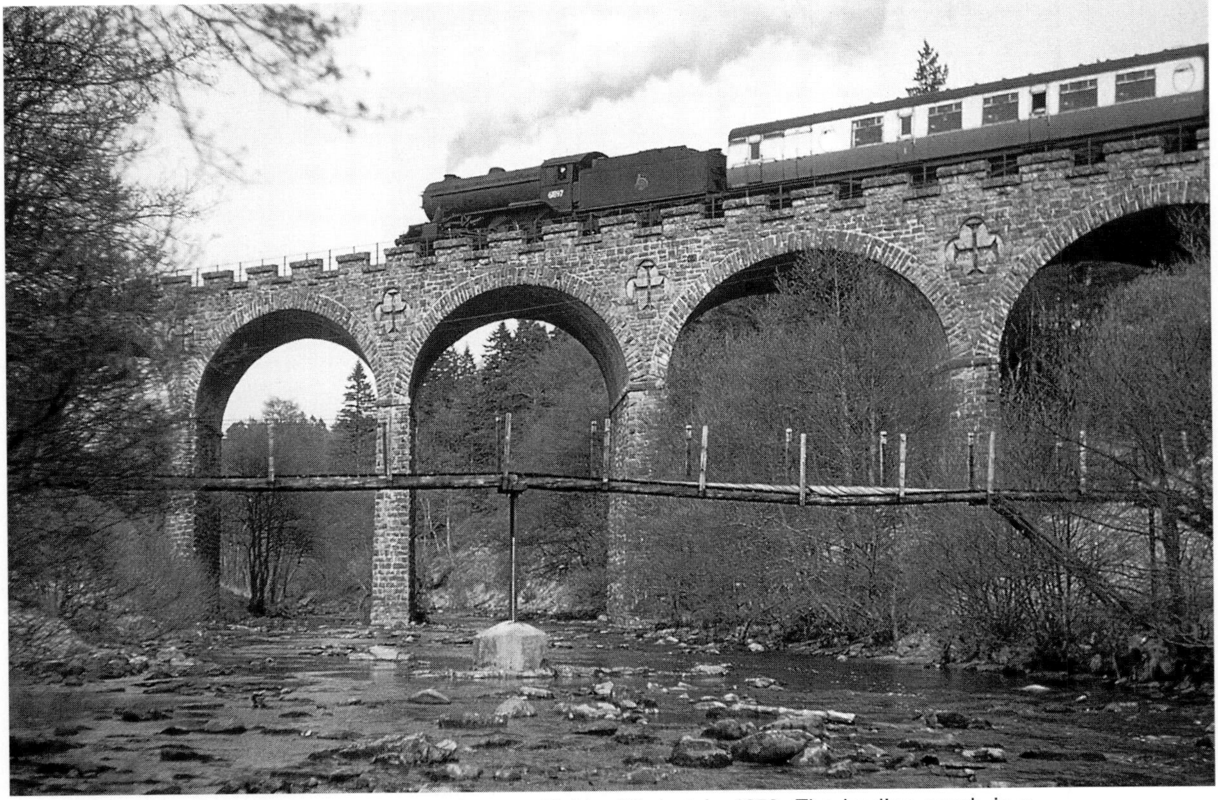

Class K3 No 61897 hauling a passenger train over Kielder Viaduct in 1953. The leading coach is a Thompson composite in 'blood-and-custard' livery. *(Colour Rail)*

Table 64

HEXHAM and RICCARTON JUNCTION

Summer 1956

Miles	WEEKDAYS		A	SO	B	B	SO
			am	am	am	pm	pm
	59 Newcastle	dep	5 52	9 45	11 10	4 27	8 20
				am	pm		
—	**HEXHAM**	dep	**6 58**	**10 39**	**12 6**	**5 16**	**9 15**
5	Humshaugh	,,	7 12	10 50	12 20	5 30	..
6¼	Chollerton	,,	7 17	10 54	12 24	5 34	....
7½	Barrasford	,,	7 21	..	12 28	5 38	9 34
11¼	Wark................	,,	7 30	11 4	12 36	5 46	9 42
15¼	**Reedsmouth** ..	arr	**7 38**	**11 12**	**12 44**	**5 54**	**9 50**
		dep	**7 46**	**11 19**	**12 48**	**6X 1**	**9 55**
17	Bellingham (North Tyne)	,,	7 51	11 24	12 53	6X 7	10 0
20½	Tarset	,,	7 58	11 31	1 0	6X13	10 6
21¾	Thorneyburn	,,	8 2	11 35	1 4	6X17	10 10
25¼	Falstone	,,	8 10	11 43	1 13	6X25	10 18
30½	Plashetts	,,	8 20	11 53	1 23	6X35	10 28
32	Lewiefield Halt	,,	8 26	11 58	1 28	6X40	10 33
33¾	Kielder Forest	,,	8 34	12 5	1 35	6X47	10 41
36¼	Deadwater	,,	8 40	—	1 41	....	—
39½	Saughtree	,,	..	..	1b48	..	..
42	**RICCARTON JUNC.**	arr	**8 50**	....	1c51	**7X 2**	....
55	Hawick	arr	10 45	..	2z17	7X27	..
107¾	Edinburgh (Waverley)	,,	12p26	....	4 27	10 25	....

Miles	WEEKDAYS		B	A	SO	SX B	SO B
			am	am	pm	pm	pm
	Edinburgh (Waverley)	dep	....	6 38	....	2 33	2 33
	Hawick	,,	6 15	8 55	..	4 32	4 32
—	**RICCARTON JUNC.**	dep	**6 47**	**10 22**	....	**5 3**	**5 5**
2½	Saughtree	,,	..	..	..	5Z 8	5L10
5¾	Deadwater	,,	6E55	10 32	....	5y13	5 17
8¼	Kielder Forest	,,	7 3	10 38	1 40	5y19	5 22
10	Lewiefield Halt	,,	7 8	10 43	1 46	5y24	5 27
11½	Plashetts	,,	7 11	10 47	1 51	5y28	5 31
16¾	Falstone	,,	7 20	10 56	2 0	5y36	5 40
20¼	Thorneyburn	,,	7 27	11 3	2 7	5y43	5 47
21½	Tarset	,,	7 31	11 7	2 11	5y48	5 51
25	Bellingham (North Tyne)	,,	7 38	11 14	2 18	5y55	5 58
26¾	**Reedsmouth** ..	arr	**7 42**	**11 18**	**2 22**	**5y59**	**6 2**
		dep	**7 48**	**11 21**	**2 26**	**6 4**	**6 4**
30¾	Wark	,,	7 57	11 30	2 35	6 13	6 13
34½	Barrasford	,,	8 4	11 37	2 42	6 20	6 20
35¾	Chollerton	,,	8 8	11 41	2 46	6 24	6 24
37	Humshaugh	,,	8 13	11 45	2 50	6 28	6 28
42	**HEXHAM**	arr	**8 27**	**11 58**	**3 3**	**6 41**	**6 41**
62¾	59 Newcastle	arr	9 7	1K10	3 48	8G 2	8G 2

A—Through Train between Newcastle and Riccarton Junction.
B—Through Train between Newcastle and Hawick.
E—Calls when required to take up on informing the Station Master at Riccarton Junction before 5 pm the day previous to travel.
G—Passengers can arrive Newcastle 7.21 pm by changing at Hexham, (depart 6.48 pm.)
K—Passengers can arrive Newcastle 12.44 pm by changing at Hexham (depart 12.5 pm).
L—Calls to set down only.
SO—Saturdays only.
SX—Saturdays excepted.
X—2 mins. later on Saturdays.
Z—Calls on Mondays and Thursdays to set down only.
b—Calls to take up only on Mondays, Thursdays and Saturdays.
c—On Mondays, Thursdays and Saturdays arrives Riccarton 1.53 pm.
p—pm.
y—1 min. later on Mondays and Thursdays.
z—On Mondays and Thursdays arrives Hawick 2.20 and on Saturdays 2.22 pm.

The Passenger Train Service from and to **Wall** has been **withdrawn.** A service of buses operated by Moffits Motor Services is available.

The Wansbeck Valley Railway

As noted above, with a strong interest in the Border Counties Railway to Hexham, the NBR was keen to develop an independent BCR route to Newcastle; the Wansbeck Valley Railway offered this opportunity. The WVR scheme received Parliamentary approval on 8 August 1859. At Morpeth the junction with the Blyth & Tyne was laid for through running to Newcastle, so Wansbeck trains reversed when entering or leaving the station. This arrangement, which included a bridge over the NER, continued until 1872, when an NBR/NER-financed curve was built into the NER station. Although single-track, bridges (but not earthworks) were built for two tracks. Beyond Morpeth the railway - affectionately known as the 'Wanny' - meandered through undulating farmland to Scotsgap, climbing for long stretches at 1 in 67½ after Angerton. Beyond Scotsgap the climb continued over the moors to Knowesgate, mostly at 1 in 70/71. The *Newcastle Chronicle* report of the opening (1865) noted: 'after passing Knowe's Gate the country assumes a bolder character, heath-covered hills, with numerous boulders peeping through the purple mantle ... sheep and black cattle dot the landscape, the latter, unacquainted apparently with the wonders of steam, scampering wildly off on the approach of the train.' After reaching nearly 850ft at Summit Cottages, a three-mile 1 in 62 descent led to Woodburn. The falling gradient continued to Reedsmouth. The line tended to follow the contours to reduce engineering expense. No tunnels or viaducts were needed. However the curvature and gradients ensured that this route could never compete with the Newcastle-Edinburgh East Coast main line; moreover the NRB/B&T route was thirteen miles longer. Morpeth-Scotsgap passenger services began on 23 July 1862 (using NBR locomotives and stock), extending to Knowesgate in October 1863, and Reedsmouth on 1 May 1865. In 1864 the NBR absorbed the Wansbeck Railway (Valley having been dropped from the name).

Meldon in April 1977. The former Wansbeck Railway station building, solidly built and unpretentious, sits comfortably in the Northumbrian landscape.
(Alan Young)

Five weeks before the complete closure of the Scotsgap-Rothbury line, a special passenger train to Rothbury passes Angerton behind Ivatt 2-6-0 No 43129 on 29 September 1963. Regular passenger services to Rothbury (and Angerton) ceased in 1952.
(Martin Bairstow Collection)

In 1863 the NBR obtained consent to use NER tracks between Hexham and Newcastle, so the strategic advantage of the Wansbeck/B&T scheme disappeared. The NBR could have left the 10-mile Knowesgate-Reedsmouth line incomplete, but they went ahead, looking to local mines and farms, and the sparse population, for traffic. Plans were changed to install a south, rather then north, facing junction at Reedsmouth, acknowledging that traffic would be to and from Hexham, rather than Scotland. Between Woodburn and Reedsmouth a branch led to Broomhope, and sidings served Hindhaugh and Craig quarries. Broomhope quarries belonged to Sir William Armstrong. Minerals were carried within the quarries on a network of lines, and the branch enabled products to travel to Armstrong's engineering works at Elswick. Quarrying ceased in 1879, after which the company -a major armaments manufacturer - used the area for weapons testing. The branch carried armaments until closure in 1963. Two quarries contributed traffic at Woodburn. Between Knowesgate and Woodburn, Siddlehill Colliery (closed c1920) tramway connected with an exchange siding. Elsdon Quarry sent stone to Knowesgate via a 3ft gauge railway from 1880 until 1915. East of Knowesgate, Whitehill Quarry contributed traffic to sidings via a tramway from the early 1900s. Between the wars it closed and the

sidings accommodated troop trains. A siding served Marycastle Quarry, again with a tramway link. From 1862-72 Mitford Quarry (Meldon/Morpeth) had a siding. Livestock traffic was also important on the Wansbeck line.

In 1863, three weekday and two Sunday trains plied between Morpeth and Scotsgap, a 35-minute journey, extending to Knowesgate and Reedsmouth (without a Sunday service) when they opened. In 1870 Scotsgap became the junction for Rothbury. Within a few years Morpeth-Rothbury trains were introduced, relegating Scotsgap-Reedsmouth to branch status. Three Scotsgap-Reedsmouth trains each way (four on Tuesdays: Hexham market day) continued until World War II; thereafter only two ran. In the 1930s scenic circular tours visited the line. With the development of Otterburn and Redesdale training areas after World War I, troop trains provided an increasing proportion of traffic on the 'Wanny', and freight traffic included military stores and artillery, was handled at Knowesgate and Woodburn. Locomotives used on the line were NBR Class R (LNER D51), D (J33), and C (J36) by 1900, and G5 and J21 in LNER/BR days, based at Rothbury. Passenger traffic was always light, one coach sufficing for most services. By 1951 it had dwindled to an unsustainable level.

Knowesgate on 20 September 1952, a week after regular passenger services were withdrawn, seen from a Newbiggin-Bellingham excursion. (J W Armstrong Trust)

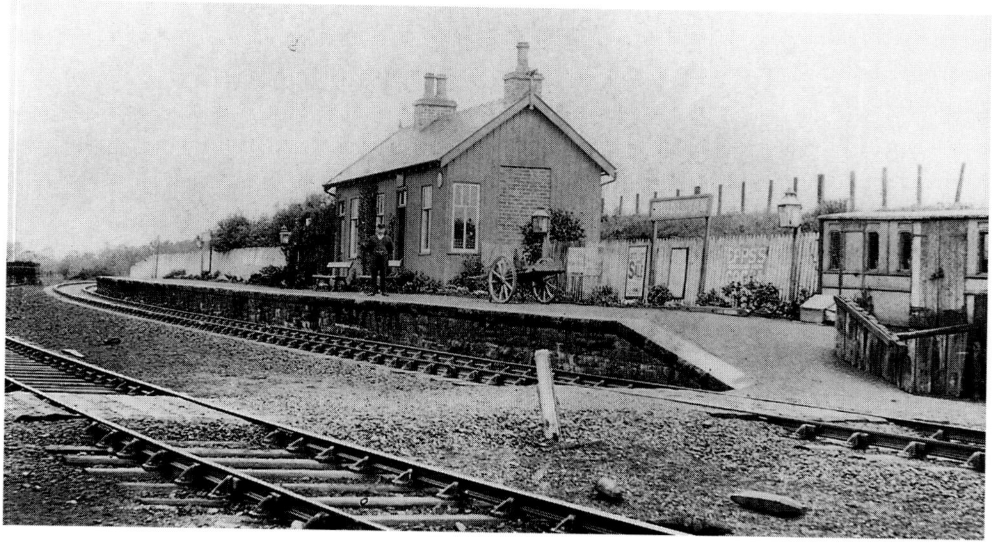

Middleton (later renamed Middleton North) c1910. The austere wooden station building is supplemented by a former passenger coach: a type of inexpensive structure also favoured by the Great Eastern Railway.
(Alan Young Collection)

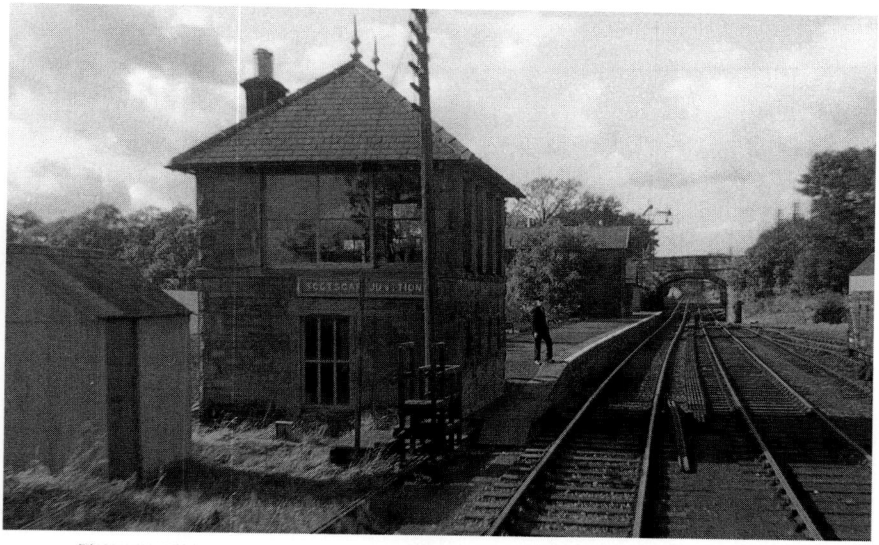

Scotsgap from a departing dmu looking towards Woodburn, with the Rothbury branch diverging to the right beyond the road bridge.
(John Birkbeck)

Table 71 MORPETH, SCOTSGAP and REEDSMOUTH and ROTHBURY *Summer 1952*

Miles	WEEKDAYS		am	am	pm	pm	
	3 Newcastle............	dep	9 28	....	5 6	....	....
—	**MORPETH**	dep	**10 10**	..	**5 50**	..	..
5½	Meldon................	,,	10 22	....	6 3	....	....
7¾	Angerton	,,	10 29	..	6 9	..	..
9½	Middleton North........	,,	10 34	....	6 14	....	....
11¼	**Scotsgap** (for Cambo) ..	arr	**10 40**	..	**6 20**	..	..
—	**Scotsgap** (for Cambo)	dep	....	**10 46**	....	**6 27**	....
14¾	Knowesgate	,,	..	10 55	..	6 38	..
21½	Woodburn...........	,,	....	11 8	....	6 52	....
25¼	**Reedsmouth**	arr	..	**11 15**	..	**7 0**	..
—	**Scotsgap** (for Cambo) ..	dep	**10 43**	....	**6 22**	....	....
14½	Longwitton	,,	10 52	..	6 31	..	..
16½	Ewesley...............	,,	10 57	....	6 38	....	....
17¾	Fontburn Halt	,,	11 2	..	6 43	..	..
22	Brinkburn Halt	,,	11 12	....	6A52	....	....
24¼	**ROTHBURY**	arr	**11 18**	..	**6 58**	..	..

Miles	WEEKDAYS		am	am	pm	pm	
—	**ROTHBURY**	dep	..	**7 51**	Bellingham (dep 4.5 pm)	**4 30**	..
2¼	Brinkburn Halt	,,	....	7 56		4 35	....
6½	Fontburn Halt	,,	..	8 7		4 46	..
7¾	Ewesley................	,,	....	8 10		4 49	....
9¾	Longwitton	,,	..	8 16		4 55	..
13	**Scotsgap** (for Cambo) ..	arr	....	**8 22**		**5 1**	....
—	**Reedsmouth**	dep	**7 44**	..	**4 15**	..	..
3¾	Woodburn...........	,,	7 54	....	4 24	....	....
10½	Knowesgate	,,	8 9	..	4 39	..	..
14	**Scotsgap** (for Cambo)	arr	**8 18**	....	**4 48**	....	....
—	**Scotsgap** (for Cambo) ..	dep	..	**8 25**	..	**5 2**	..
15	Middleton North........	,,	....	8 29	....	5 6	....
16½	Angerton	,,	..	8 34	..	5 10	..
18¾	Meldon................	,,	....	8 40	....	5 15	....
24¼	**MORPETH**	arr	..	**8 51**	..	**5 25**	..
40¾	3 Newcastle............	arr	....	9 29	....	6 12	....

A—Calls to set down only.

	'Traffic' 1880	Tickets issued 1951
Meldon	8,488	644
Angerton	6,925	291
Middleton	4,504	no data
Scotsgap	8,286	607
Knowesgate	4,507	237
Woodburn	7,508	1,108

Withdrawal of Wansbeck Valley and Rothbury passenger trains in 1952 coincided with the closure of Rothbury and Reedsmouth sheds. Replacement buses were operated by Messrs. Batty (Morpeth-Scotsgap-Cambo) and Tait (Morpeth-Knowegate-Kirkwhelpington). Goods trains were withdrawn west of Woodburn and on the Rothbury branch in 1963. Military traffic (goods and passenger) was the lifeblood of the remaining Morpeth-Woodburn line. Blyth-based J27 0-6-0s and Class 25 diesels hauled these trains.

From 1964-66 Gosforth Round Table took a lively interest in the branch, dubbing it the Heatherbell Line, 'England's northernmost, Scottishmost, forgottennmost branch line that no-one remembered to close'. They chartered dmus for the *Bellingham Belle* (19 September 1964, repeated a year later), and the *Wood Burner* (1 July 1966). Foot-and-Mouth Disease thwarted plans for a September 1966 trip, but the *Wansbeck Piper* ran on 2 October 1966, the day before complete closure. This eleven-coach train was hauled by two LM 4MT 2-6-0 engines,

coupled back-to-back. I travelled on the 1964 *Bellingham Belle* and 1966 *Wansbeck Piper*. The *Piper* trip was on a sunny autumn afternoon. Photographic stops were made at Angerton and Scotsgap, their platforms overwhelmed by many of the 645 passengers. The sound of the engines struggling up the gradient into the moorland, the smell of steam, and the sight of sunlight diffusing through it are abiding memories. At intervals photographers appeared in the heather, recording the historic moment; others in cars raced the train, seeking vantage points to view the event. Sheep on the line caused two unscheduled stops. Thirty-seven minutes at Woodburn was sufficient time to explore the remaining section of track towards Reedsmouth, and scale the rickety signal-post to view the locomotives as they ran round the train. It was a sad moment when, at 17.00, the train departed to the strains of a piper playing a lament, and exploding detonators. A steam-hauled demolition train soon dismantled the last length of Scottish railway in England. Much of the trackbed and most station sites are well preserved.

Stations
The stations stood in thinly populated countryside, perhaps with one or two farms in sight. However at Scotsgap, a community grew at the junction, with a livestock mart (still in use) and temperance hotel. Station buildings at Meldon, Angerton, Knowesgate and Woodburn remain in residential use.

J27 0-6-0 No 65834 with the branch goods at Woodburn in April 1963.   *(John Birkbeck)*

Meldon station's 70yd platform north of the track had a substantial stone building. The stationmaster's accommodation was in a simple, but attractive, two-storey structure at right angles to the platform, with the adjoining single-storey office section set back. At the east end stood a signal box, with sidings serving a coal depot and goods warehouse. A further siding south of the running-line permitted trains to pass.

Angerton. East of the level crossing, the platform was north of the track and possessed a building like that at Meldon but with an additional single-storey wing beyond the offices. Adjacent were an elderly coach body, serving as a store, and a hut containing the ground-frame. The platform was originally on a loop line, but before 1896 track reorganisation put the platform (lengthened to 100yd) on the running-line.

Middleton was renamed Middleton North by the LNER in 1923, avoiding confusion with their stations in Yorkshire and Norfolk. The station stood in North Middleton 'township'. The original 40yd passenger platform was east of the road-bridge and north of the running-line, and a loop extended westwards. Site constrictions prevented platform lengthening, so a new one, some 90yd long, was built west of the bridge. A small, plain wooden building was provided. The loop was eventually reduced to a siding. By 1964 the building had disappeared. Nothing remains of the station.

Scotsgap was variously known as Scot's Gap (*Bradshaw* until 1903), Scotsgap (for Cambo) by BR, and Scotsgap Jct on the nameboard. The original layout comprised a single 65yd (later increased to 120yd) platform south of the running-line, an Angerton-style building, and sidings on the Morpeth side. Before 1895 a signal box was added at the platform's east end. A goods platform faced the passenger platform across the sidings, and adjoined a goods warehouse. The station building survives as commercial premises, extending onto the trackbed.

Knowesgate (Knowe's Gate until 1908) was named after an adjacent house, and served Kirkwhelpington. Originally a single short platform south of the running-line and a loop were installed. Both were later extended, the platform to 80yd. A goods dock was constructed on the loop. The austere, single-storey stone building had a gable facing the platform, and booking/waiting facilities were in an adjacent wood and glass-fronted section. The building remains little altered.

Parsons Platform. Sir Charles Parsons, the industrialist, owned Ray Demesne, a large country house near the railway. A short platform was constructed for his convenience. After his death (1931) estate staff and their families continued to use the facility. The platform was used in 1937 but abandoned before 1952. (The NBR called the platform Ray House.)

Summit Cottages had no platform, but trains called at this remote location for railway employees. Their wives used the trains for Saturday shopping trips.

Woodburn station - shown on the front cover - served West Woodburn and Otterburn. The platform was northwest of the running-line. A parallel siding for mineral traffic was extended into a loop by 1895, and a signal box was built about 1890. From about 1893-1906 Woodburn was the terminus of a contractor's railway to Catcleugh, where a dam was under construction. Sidings and a goods platform were northeast of the passenger facilities. The station building was a plain, single-storey affair with a wood and glass-fronted booking/waiting area. This is beautifully maintained as a house, with the trackbed and platform incorporated into its garden.

Vickers Platform. A 43yd timber platform was constructed on the east side at Broomhope branch junction. Trains made unadvertised stops 'by arrangement' from about 1880, for workers at the armaments testing area and local residents, and called until 1952. The Vickers company maintained the platform and lighting.

Station Master Jefferson attends to the one passenger train of the year at Woodburn on 19 September 1964. At other times he was kept busy by the modest goods traffic here and at Scotsgap. *(John Birkbeck)*

The Rothbury Branch

Early, unsuccessful schemes for rail access to Rothbury village would have linked it with Morpeth (1855) and Acklington (1856). In 1862 three distinguished supporters of the Wansbeck scheme - Richard Hodgson, Earl Grey, and Sir W C Trevelyan - threw their weight behind the Northumberland Central Railway project for a Scotsgap-Rothbury-Wooler-Cornhill line. Royal Assent was obtained on 28 July 1863. The NBR had, by then, absorbed the Wansbeck line. Various financial complications delayed construction of the Northumberland Central. In the meantime the decision was reached to abandon the Rothbury-Cornhill section, but to seek an extension of the time allowed to complete to Rothbury; both were agreed by Parliament in April 1867. The passenger service started on 1 October 1870, using NBR stock. The NCR was in serious debt. The reduction of the through route to a branch with little earning potential dulled the NBR's enthusiasm to acquire the line. Nevertheless, on 1 February 1872, the NBR absorbed the NCR. Ten years later the Central Northumberland Railway project (supported by the NBR) to extend from Rothbury to Wooler came before Parliament, but the alternative NER Alnwick-Wooler-Coldstream proposals were preferred and approved. So Rothbury remained the terminus. Any NBR intentions to gain more ground in Northumberland were abandoned. The NBR's special relationship with the Blyth & Tyne had already ceased when, in 1874, the latter was absorbed by the NER.

The 13-mile Scotsgap-Rothbury branch was built as single track, but sufficient land was purchased for doubling, should the need arise. It crossed hilly terrain, requiring steep gradients, numerous curves, and substantial earthworks. A 50-foot embankment at Forestburn, and a deep cutting at Thrum Mill near Rothbury, were constructed. A twelve-arch viaduct, about 60ft high (and still intact) crossed Font Burn. From Scotsgap there was a 1 in 75 climb to the 694ft

J27 0-6-0 No 65833 passing Longwitton on 26 May 1961 with the pick-up goods from Rothbury
(Geoffrey C Lewthwaite)

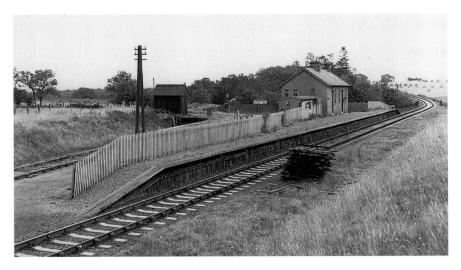

Ewesley was typical of the intermediate stations on the Rothbury branch, modestly equipped and serving sparsely populated countryside. Unusually, in the 1880s the North British appointed a Station Mistress to this remote spot.
(Martin Bairstow Collection)

summit at Longwitton, and Brinkburn-Rothbury included a 1 in 60 descent.

The branch carried the limited quantities of passenger and goods traffic offered by the thinly populated countryside, and a growing number of holidaymakers. Rothbury became a 'health resort' and the picturesque landscape traversed by the railway was one of the delights of a visit to the village. For a couple of years Scotsgap-Rothbury operated as a branch from the Morpeth-Reedsmouth line, but a pattern of three weekday Morpeth-Rothbury trains each way (with connections for Reedsmouth at Scotsgap) taking about an hour became standard until World War II. Two coaches generally sufficed, or a single coach in the final years; however, longer trains operated in summer, and for meetings at Rothbury racecourse. In the 1920s-30s a through carriage operated between Newcastle and Rothbury. *Bradshaw* (July 1938) shows such carriages departing Rothbury at 8.5 am, 7.22 pm (Saturdays excepted) and 8.28 pm (Saturdays only) and arriving at Rothbury at 3.19 and 6.51 pm. The same timetable includes two Sunday trains each way. Early in World War II the service was reduced to two Morpeth-Scotsgap returns per day, and Sunday trains ceased. However by 1942, and until 1950, a Saturday train left Rothbury at 11.30 am, arriving back at 3.19 pm. At closure, only two trains ran each day. Passenger trains were hauled by the same classes of engines as on the Scotsgap-Reedsmouth line.

Goods traffic

Several quarries and mines depended on the Rothbury branch. Between Scotsgap and Longwitton a siding served Hartington quarries. At Longwitton, Greenleighton Quarry northwest of the station and a colliery to the southeast each had sidings and provided traffic until the 1880s. At Fontburn, Whitehouse siding was installed in 1883-84 serving a lime-kiln, and was connected by tramways to Ewesley Quarry to the east and a coal drift mine to the north (opened in the late 1880s). Both closed by 1900. In the 1890s a 3ft gauge contractor's line was built to carry materials to Fontburn Reservoir construction site. Further north, at Forestburn a branch served a colliery and quarry east of the line during the 1920s; and Brinkburn Colliery, also to the east, was served by a siding and tramway until 1926. Finally at Brinkburn station sidings, an aerial ropeway brought coal from Healeycotes 1¾ miles east from about 1920 until the 1940s. Livestock traffic was important. At Scotsgap and Rothbury marts were opened near the stations after the railway arrived. In World War II, moors near Rothbury were used for military training, for which the branch carried supplies.

Closure

In 1951 only 2,603 tickets were issued at Rothbury; figures are unavailable for the other stations on the branch. Regular passenger services were withdrawn in 1952, but steam-hauled and dmu excursions continued to use the branch. A farewell steam-hauled excursion visited Rothbury on 9 November 1963, two days before goods services ended. Within a year the tracks were removed.

Stations

All stations, except Fontburn, opened with the line in 1870, although Longwitton was originally untimetabled. With the exception of the terminus, stations had small, inexpensive buildings. The contrast with the NER's palatial premises at equally quiet and remote stations between Alnwick and Coldstream is striking.

Longwitton, at first called Rothley, opened as a private halt for the Trevelyan estates. It became a public station in 1873. In April 1875 it was renamed after a hamlet three miles away. The 70yd platform was on the up side of the line. The utilitarian wooden building with hipped roof reflected the limited funds available for construction; it contained the usual booking and waiting facilities. In later years an old coach body was installed for storage. Goods were handled, and the changing layout of sidings reflected the fortunes of the local mineral workings. In 1973 the platform, building and old coach were still in place, but they have since been removed.

Ewesley was within an ancient earthwork, immediately west of a bridge over the Scotsgap-Rothbury road. The 90yd platform on the up side had a wooden building like that at Middleton North, so it was probably an 1880s/90s addition. A small brick-built station house stood back from the platform, and the house and fragments of the platform still survive. A goods siding and dock stood at the Rothbury end, and a lengthy siding southwest of the running-line allowed trains to pass. When Fontburn's goods facilities closed on 2 January 1922, Font Siding (formerly serving the reservoir construction site) and Whitehouse Siding (for Ewesley Quarry) were transferred to Ewesley station to control: thus the confusing naming on LNER network maps, 'Fontburn Halt and Ewesley Goods'.

Fontburn. Research by Harold Bowtell has revealed the fascinating history of this minor station. Trains possibly called unofficially by 1896 for workers at Whitehouse Quarry and lime-works and for occupants of railway cottages. From 1901-09 construction of Fontburn Reservoir required the establishment of a temporary 'shanty-town' beside the railway for about 450 people. Various 3ft-gauge lines served the construction site, and associated sidings were added to the Rothbury branch. The NBR provided a passenger station, west of the track, with an 80yd timber platform, waiting shed and booking office. It opened on 12 January 1903 as a 'Temporary Platform at Whitehouse Siding' for workmen. *Bradshaw* included the new station, but removed it when the Board of Trade complained that it had not been inspected. Duly inspected, Whitehouse was reinstated. On 1 May 1904 it was renamed Fontburn to avoid confusion with Whitehouse, Aberdeenshire.

Fontburn Halt on 13 September 1952 seen from the 4.30 pm Rothbury-Morpeth train, the last regular up train. Three passengers are alighting at this desolate spot.
(J W Armstrong Trust)

Brinkburn on 4 June 1963. At this time goods trains still used the line, but they ceased five months later.
(Alan Young)

The demolition contractors have moved in at Rothbury with their own small diesel locomotive. The loco shed (right) had closed with the ending of the passenger service in September 1952.
(John Birkbeck)

After the construction workers dispersed the station was retained, but it closed on 3 October 1921. Following a local petition it reopened, unstaffed, on 21 November 1921 as Fontburn Halt. The nameboard was altered accordingly. Passengers obtained tickets from the guard or at Scotsgap or Rothbury stations. Ewesley's stationmaster took charge of the halt. Nothing remains of the halt today.

Brinkburn was perched on a hillside, reached by a narrow road from the east and a moorland path from the west. The 70yd platform east of the track, had a larger version of the Ewesley building, and two tiny sheds. The station house was separate. Goods and coal were handled immediately northeast of the passenger station. From September 1948 it was unstaffed and renamed Brinkburn Halt. There is now little evidence at the site that it was a station.

Rothbury had a single 200yd platform on the up side for passenger traffic. The H-plan wooden building was probably erected by the NBR. The twin pavilions facing the platform, and intervening recess, were behind a flat awning with saw-tooth valance. There was no stationmaster's house. A double loop adjoined the running-line, which ended at a turntable. Clusters of sidings were installed north, south, and east of the passenger facilities, the northern group having a goods dock that backed onto the passenger platform. The eastern sidings were for carriages. Rothbury had a signal box at the east end of the platform, whilst intermediate stations (and Forestburn Siding) had only ground-frames. A wooden engine-shed stood opposite the passenger platform, entered by a track from the turntable. It was built in 1872 and could accommodate two locomotives. In 1924 its occupants were a D51 tank and a J36 freight (both ex-NBR) and in 1939 a G5 for passenger traffic and J21 for freight (both ex-NER). In October 1915 the shed was damaged by fire and rebuilt, slightly smaller, in brick. By the early 1970s an industrial estate occupied the station site.

Reedsmouth, looking towards Hexham on 15 September 1956, with a train for Hawick in the platform. The Morpeth line is behind the signal box.
(Geoffrey C Lewthwaite)

Gosforth Round Table chartered a dmu on 19 September 1964 for the Bellingham Belle from Newcastle to Woodburn. A coach connection was provided to the Bellingham Show. *(John Birkbeck)*

Minor Railways

The total length of waggonways and freight lines probably exceeded the 300 miles of passenger railways in Northumberland. It is impossible to calculate their total extent. The earliest waggonways pre-dated accurate mapping, and some existed for a very short time. Railway systems of various gauges existed within quarries and collieries, above and below ground, their layouts adjusted as working faces were developed or abandoned. Many miles of contractors' lines, to convey materials to reservoir construction sites, existed for only a few years. Some minor lines have been described with the passenger lines to which they connected; others are described below.

Reservoir Lines

Harold Bowtell's *Dam Builders' Railways from Durham's Dales to the Border* (1994) is highly recommended for its detailed survey of this subject.

Catcleugh

The most ambitious project was associated with the construction of Newcastle & Gateshead Water Company's Catcleugh Reservoir in Redesdale, between 1893 and 1906. A fourteen-mile 3ft gauge light railway connected Woodburn station yard with Catcleugh to carry pipes, stone, and clay to the construction site. At least eight locomotives were employed. Woodburn sidings were extended to handle traffic such as cement from Willington Quay via the NER and NBR. The Catcleugh line was engineered to minimise earthworks, however wooden trestle bridges were required, including one approaching viaduct proportions over Brig Burn (Corsenside). From Otterburn to Catcleugh the line accompanied the modern A68 road, parts of which have been realigned on the railway's course. A two-mile branch from Redesdale Arms climbed to Yatefield clay pits. Additional stretches of light railway were installed southward from Woodburn to Woodfield Bridge (Barrasford) in connection with the building of Catcleugh pipeline.

Because of the remote location, the workforce lived in two temporary hut-villages at Catcleugh, named Newcastle and Gateshead - appropriately, the former north of the River Rede, and the latter to the south! In 1899 the population rose to over 500 adults and children. An informal passenger service operated on the line, offering a bumpy ride between Catcleugh and Woodburn in open waggons or 4-wheel saloon coaches. Photographic evidence exists of a 'kiddies' special' on the route. Passengers had to walk 500yd between Riverside Meadow on the Catcleugh line and Woodburn station; it was considered hazardous for them to travel on the incline between these points. Some goods traffic was also carried, including wool from a local farm. When the reservoir was complete the line was no longer needed; final train movements took place in 1906. A few traces of the line remain, including earthworks near Miller Burn (Corsenside).

Whittle Dean

This group of reservoirs is three miles northwest of Wylam. Works to extend them coincided with the Catcleugh scheme. Between about 1892 and 1905 a nine-mile 3ft gauge light railway operated between Horsley Wood, on the north bank of the Tyne, one mile northwest of North Wylam, and Ryal. Three Hudswell Clarke 0-4-0 saddle tanks hauled the waggons. The NER installed a siding just west of West Wylam Junction from which construction materials reached Horsley Wood via a 600yd aerial ropeway across the river. The NER also assisted the project by providing a morning and evening workmen's train serving North Wylam. A short embankment near the A69 is about the only visible evidence of the former railway.

0-6-0T No 45 at Shilbottle Colliery on 31 August 1972. The colliery branch joined the East Coast main line about 11/2 miles south of Alnmouth.
(Tom Heavyside)

Kielder Water - if only!

The development of Kielder Water - Britain's largest artificial lake - was supported by road, not by rail. Seventy years after Catcleugh, Fontburn, and other such projects, the road system and capacity of road vehicles had improved enormously. However, had the Border Counties line been in place in the late 1970s, it could have spared local communities the irritation of heavy lorries, laden with construction materials, pounding the country lanes. The Border Counties could also have been a scenic and environmentally acceptable means of conveying some of the many tourists to Kielder Water, and conecting with the steamer 'Osprey'.

Tourist Lines

Woodhorn Colliery Museum has a 2ft gauge line with two Hunslet diesel locomotives formerly at Vane Tempest Colliery (Seaham).

The Heatherslaw Railway opened in July 1989. This 15in gauge line, some eight miles northwest of Wooler, follows the River Till for 1¾ miles from Heatherslaw to Etal, an attractive 'estate village'. The southern terminus is at Heatherslaw Mill, a tourist and interpretive centre. The station here has a timber pitched-roof trainshed and extremely low platforms. Coaches are hauled by **Lady Augusta,** an 0-4-2 solid fuel-burning locomotive, or by the stand-by bogie diesel engine, **Clive.**

Other Lines

Trains conveyed miners between Killingworth station and **Seaton Burn Colliery** along lines otherwise reserved for coal traffic; the dates of operation are uncertain. The neighbouring **Hazelrigg Colliery** also had miners' trains until 1955. **North Walbottle Colliery** was similarly served, until 1968, by a branch from the North Wylam line. **Kirkheaton Colliery's** short-lived informal service from the Darras Hall branch is described in *Suburban Railways of Tyneside.* Elsewhere, in rural Northumberland, there were freight lines where passengers might have been carried unofficially.

On **Holy Island** two waggonways existed to transport limestone and ironstone. One connected Castle Point and the Links, along the east coast, and is now a footpath. The other went from the Links to Chare End, where the causeway begins.

A three-mile light railway, shown on the One-inch Ordnance Survey map of 1947 carried timber from **Detchant Wood** to a sawmill adjacent to the A1 road at Middleton Hall.

At **Ross Links** near Bamburgh the O.S. One-inch map of 1956 shows a system of three linked branches terminating in loops. This is believed to have served a World War II firing range.

From **Unthank** to Tweedmouth a three-mile waggonway, including an inclined plane, carried coal as early as 1764.

By 1809 **Shilbottle Colliery** was sending coal to Bondgate, Alnwick, by a waggonway.

Heatherslaw Mill on 18 August 2001. 0-4-2 *Lady Augusta* prepares to leave for the short journey to Etal.
(Alan Young)

Bibliography

Bowtell H D	*Dam Builders' Railways from Durham's Dales to the Border*	(Plateway Press 1994)
Fawcett W	*North Eastern Railway Architecture Vol. 1*	(NERA 2001)
Jenkins S C	*The Alston Branch*	(Oakwood 1991)
Jenkins S C	*The Rothbury Branch*	(Oakwood 1991
Quick M E	*Railway Passenger Stations in England, Scotland and Wales*	(R & CHS 2002)
Sewell GWM	*The North British Railway in Northumberland*	(Merlin 1991)
Stobbs A	*Memories of the LNER: Rural Northumberland*	(Author 1992)
Tomlinson WW	*The North Eastern Railway: Its rise and development*	(Andrew Reid 1915)
Warn C R	*Main Line Railways of Northumberland*	(Frank Graham 1976)
Warn C R	*Railways of the Northumberland Coalfield*	(Frank Graham 1976)
Warn C R	*Waggonways & Early Railways of Northumberland*	(Frank Graham 1976)
Warn C R	*Rural Branch Lines of Northumberland*	(Frank Graham 1978)
Wells J A	*The Blyth & Tyne Railway*	(Northumberland County Library 1989)
Wells J A	*The Blyth & Tyne Branch*	(Northumberland County Library 1990)
Wells J A	*Railways of Northumberland and Newcastle upon Tyne 1828-1998*	(Powdene 1998)
Whittle G	*The Newcastle & Carlisle Railway*	(David & Charles 1979)
Wright A	*The North Sunderland Railway*	(Oakwood 1988)
-	*North Eastern Express*	(N.E.R.A. various editions)

Alston station on 11 August 1991, restored for narrow gauge trains. 0-6-0 No 10 *Naklo*, built in 1957, previously worked at a sugar factory near Bydgoszcz in Poland.   *(Martin Bairstow)*

Appendices

Station names as at present or at passenger closure.
Absence of Closed (Goods) date = no goods service, or not known.

¶ Untimetabled station, halt, or stopping place.
* Complicated history: see text for more details

Newcastle - Berwick-upon-Tweed
(East Coast Main Line)

Opened

Newcastle (Carliol Square) - Heaton - Shields	20.6.1839
Heaton Junction - Morpeth	1.3.1847
Chathill - Tweedmouth	29.3.1847
Morpeth - Chathill	1.7.1847
Tweedmouth - Berwick (Goods)	20.7.1850
(Passengers)	30.8.1850
Newcastle Central (replaced Carliol Sq) – Manors	30.8.1850

Stations	Opened (Pass)	Closed (Pass)	Closed (Goods)
Newcastle Central	30.8.1850	open	
Newcastle Carliol Sq	20.6.1839	30.8.1850	
Manors East	30.8.1850	open	
Heaton (first)	By 1.1856	1.4.1887	
Heaton (second)	1.4.1887	11.8.1980	
Forest Hall	2.1856	15.9.1958	15.9.1958
Benton renamed 1.12.1874			
Killingworth	1.3.1847	15.9.1958	7.6.1965
Races traffic continued for some time after passenger closure. Parcels traffic ceased 31.10.1966			
Annitsford	8.7.1878	15.9.1958	11.11.1963
Dudley Colliery	4.1860	8.7.1878	
Dudley renamed 1.9.1874. Renamed Annitsford 5.1878?			
Cramlington	1.3.1847	open	4.7.1966
Plessey	7.1859	15.9.1958	2.4.1962
Stannington	1.3.1847	15.9.1958	10.8.1964
Netherton renamed 1.1.1892			
Morpeth	1.3.1847	open	
Pegswood	1.1.1903	open	10.8.1964
Ashington Colliery Jn	12.1871	8.1878	
Longhirst	1.7.1847	29.10.1951	10.8.1964
Widdrington	1.7.1847	open	28.12.1964
Chevington	10.1870	15.9.1958	10.8.1964
Acklington	1.7.1847	open	5.9.1966
Warkworth	1.7.1847	15.9.1958	2.4.1962
Alnmouth	1.10.1850	open	
Bilton Junction renamed 2.5.1892			
Lesbury	1.7.1847	4.1851?	
Longhoughton	1.7.1847	18.6.1962	18.6.1962
Closed (passengers) 5.5.1941 to 7.10.1946			
Little Mill	1.1861	15.9.1958	7.6.1965
Private station 1.7.1847 to 1.1861			
Closed (passengers) 5.5.1941 to 7.10.1946			
Christon Bank	1.7.1847	15.9.1958	7.6.1965
Closed (passengers) 5.5.1941 to 7.10.1946			
¶Fallodon	1.7.1847	1935	
Chathill	29.3.1847	open	7.6.1965
Newham	2.1851	25.9.1950	25.9.1950
Closed (passengers) 5.5.1941 to 7.10.1946			
Lucker	29.3.1847	2.2.1953	7.6.1965
Closed (passengers) 5.5.1941 to 7.10.1946			

Belford	29.3.1847	29.1.1968	7.6.1965
Cragg Mill	2.1871	10.1877	
Smeafield	2.1871	1.5.1930	
Continued in private use for some time after 1.5.1930			
Beal, for Holy Island	29.3.1847	29.1.1968	26.4.1965
Goswick	11.1870	15.9.1958	10.8.1964
Wind Mill Hill renamed 1.1.1898			
Closed (passengers) 5.5.1941 to 7.10.1946			
Scremerston	29.3.1847	8.7.1951	8.7.1951
Closed (passengers) 5.5.1941 to 7.10.1946			
In 1953 a Friday northbound train called for railway staff			
Tweedmouth	29.3.1847	15.6.1964	
Berwick-upon-Tweed	22.6.1846	open	4.9.1967
Berwick renamed 1.1.1955			

Chevington - Amble

Opened: Coal 5.9.1849   **Opened: Passengers** 2.1879
Closed: Passengers 7.7.1930
Closed to all traffic 6.10.1969

Stations	Opened (Pass)	Closed (Pass)	Closed (Goods)
Broomhill	2.1879	7.7.1930	4.5.1964
Amble	2.1879	7.7.1930	14.12.1964
Parcels traffic ceased at Amble on 6.10.1969			

Alnmouth - Alnwick

Opened: Goods 19.8.1850   **Opened: Passengers** 1.10.1850
Closed: Passengers 29.1.1968   **Closed: Goods** 7.10.1968

Stations	Opened (Pass)	Closed (Pass)	Closed (Goods)
Alnwick (first)	1.10.1850	5.9.1887	
Alnwick (second)	5.9.1887	29.1.1968	7.10.1968

Alnwick - Coldstream

Opened

Coldstream - Wooperton (Goods)	2.5.1887
Coldstream - Alnwick (All traffic)	5.9.1887
Closed: Passengers	22.9.1930
Closed: Goods	
Mindrum – Kirknewton (Temporary)	8.1948
Ilderton - Wooler	10.1949
Alnwick - Ilderton	2.3.1953
Wooler - Coldstream	29.3.1965

Stations	Opened (Pass)	Closed (Pass)	Closed (Goods)
Edlingham Halt	5.9.1887	22.9.1930	2.3.1953
Edlingham renamed 23.8.1926			
Goods renamed Edlingham Siding 14.2.1938			
Whittingham	5.9.1887	22.9.1930	2.3.1953
Glanton	5.9.1887	22.9.1930	2.3.1953
Hedgeley	5.9.1887	22.9.1930	2.3.1953
Wooperton	5.9.1887	22.9.1930	2.3.1953
Ilderton	5.9.1887	22.9.1930	2.3.1953
Wooler	5.9.1887	22.9.1930	29.3.1965
Akeld	5.9.1887	22.9.1930	29.3.1965
Kirknewton	5.9.1887	22.9.1930	30.3.1953
Mindrum	5.9.1887	22.9.1930	29.3.1965

Chathill - Seahouses
(North Sunderland Railway)

Opened: Goods 1.8.1898 **Opened: Passengers** 18.12.1898
Closed to all traffic 29.10.1951

Stations	Opened (Pass)	Closed (Pass)	Closed (Goods)
North Sunderland	18.12.1898?	29.10.1951	2.1928
Untimetabled until 8.1934			
Seahouses	18.12.1898	29.10.1951	29.10.1951

Tweedmouth - Kelso (-St Boswells)

Opened

Tweedmouth - Sprouston	27.7.1849
Kelso (Wallace Nick) - St Boswells	17.6.1850
Sprouston - Kelso	1.6.1851
Kelso (Maxwellheugh) – (Wallace Nick)	27.1.1851
Closed: Passengers	15.6.1964
Closed: Goods Tweedmouth - Kelso	29.3.1965
Kelso - St Boswells	30.3.1968

Stations	Opened (Pass)	Closed (Pass)	Closed (Goods)
Velvet Hall	27.7.1849	4.7.1955	29.3.1965
Norham	27.7.1849	15.6.1964	29.3.1965
Twizell	8.1861	4.7.1955	7.12.1953
Coldstream	27.7.1849	15.6.1964	29.3.1965
Cornhill renamed 1.10.1873			
Sunilaws	7.1859	4.7.1955	29.3.1965
Wark renamed 1.8.1871			
Carham	27.7.1849	4.7.1955	18.5.1964
Sprouston	27.7.1849	4.7.1955	25.1.1965
Kelso	27.1.1851	15.6.1964	30.3.1968

Blyth and Tyne system

Opened

Percy Main - Seghill	(Coal)	1.6.1840
	(Passengers)	28.8.1841
Seghill - Blyth		3.3.1847
Hartley - Seaton Sluice (Passengers)		1847
Newsham – Bedlington	(Coal)	12.6.1850
	(Passengers)	3.8.1850
Bedlington - Morpeth		1.4.1858
Bedlington - North Seaton		7.11.1859
Whitley (Monkseaton) – Hartley (Goods)		31.10.1860
	(Passengers)	1.4.1861
West Sleekburn- Cambois (Goods)		1867
North Seaton - Newbiggin		1.3.1872
Ashington Collieries link - station (Coal)		1886
Newsham - Blyth (Goods line)		1888
Marchey's House Jn - Winning Jn (Coal)		13.7.1896
Cambois Branch - North Blyth Staith		13.7.1896

Closed: Passengers:

Hartley – Seaton Sluice	1852
Whitley (Monkseaton) – Hartley	27.6.1864
Reopened 6.1904	
Bedlington - Morpeth	3.4.1950
Backworth / Monkseaton -	
Blyth / Newbiggin	2.11.1964

Closed: Goods

Woodhorn - Newbiggin	2.11.1964
Monkseaton - Hartley	2.11.1964
Blyth Signal Box - Blyth	2.11.1964
Isabella - Blyth Engine Shed	29.1.1968

Stations	Opened (Pass)	Closed (Pass)	Closed (Goods)
Percy Main (B&T)	28.8.1841	27.6.1864	
Prospect Hill	28.8.1841	27.6.1864	
Backworth	28.8.1841	27.6.1864	7.6.1965
Holywell station renamed (for passenger use) 4.1860			
¶Backworth Colliery	1914	1918	
Seghill	28.8.1841	2.11.1964	9.12.1963
Seaton Delaval	3.3.1847	2.11.1964	9.12.1963
Seaton Delaval Colliery renamed 8.1864			
Hartley Pit	3.3.1847	1851?	
Hartley	1851?	2.11.1964	9.12.1963
The Avenue	1.4.1861	27.6.1864	
Dairy House renamed later 1861.			
Used in 1870s on Sundays in summer.			
Newsham	8.1850?	2.11.1964	7.6.1965
Blyth (first)	3.3.1847	1.5.1867	
Blyth (second)	1.5.1867	2.11.1964	23.9.1963
Bebside	3.8.1850	2.11.1964	9.12.1963
Cowpen Lane renamed 4.1860			
Bedlington	3.8.1850	2.11.1964	7.9.1965
Choppington	1.4.1858	3.4.1950	9.3.1964
Hepscott	1.4.1858	3.4.1950	9.3.1964
Morpeth (B&T)	1.4.1858	24.5.1880	
North Seaton	7.11.1859	2.11.1964	9.12.1963
Ashington	6.1878	2.11.1964	3.2.1964
Hirst, for Ashington; renamed Ashington 1.10.1889			
Newbiggin	1.3.1872	2.11.1964	2.11.1964
¶Ashington Colliery	?	1964	
¶Ellington	?	1964	
¶Linton	?	1964	
¶New Moor	?	1964	

Newcastle - Carlisle (via Wylam)

Opened

Blaydon - Hexham (Goods)	late 1834
Blaydon - Hexham (Passengers)	10.3.1835
Derwenthaugh - Blaydon	11.6.1835
Hexham - Haydon Bridge	28.6.1835
Blenkinsopp Colliery - Carlisle	19.7.1836
Redheugh - Derwenthaugh	1.3.1837
Derwenthaugh - Carlisle complete	18.6.1838
Blaydon- Scotswood- Newcastle (Shot Tower)	21.10.1839
Newcastle terminus changed to Forth	1.3.1847
Newcastle terminus changed to Central	1.1.1851
Newcastle (King Edward Br South Jn) – Blaydon	4.12.1982
Closed to all traffic	
Newcastle Central – Blaydon (via Scotswood)	4.12.1982

(via North Wylam)
Opened

Scotswood - Newburn	12.7.1875
Newburn - North Wylam	13.5.1876
North Wylam - West Wylam Jn	10.1876
Closed: Passengers: Scotswood - West Wylam Jn	11.3.1968
Closed: Goods Newburn - West Wylam Jn	14.9.1967
Scotswood - Newburn	1.12.1986

Stations	Opened (Pass)	Closed (Pass)	Closed (Goods)
Newcastle Central	1.1.1851	open	
(for Newcastle & Carlisle)			
Newcastle Forth	1.3.1847	1.1.1851	
Newcastle(Shot Tower)	21.10.1839	1.3.1847	
Elswick	2.9.1889	2.1.1967	
¶Scotswood Works Halt*	1915	1947	

	Opened (Pass)	Closed (Pass)	Closed (Goods)
Scotswood (N&C plats)	21.10.1839?	3.9.1966	26.4.1965
Scotswood (SNW plats)	12.7.1875	1.5.1967	26.4.1965
Redheugh*	1.3.1837	5.1853	
Derwenthaugh	11.6.1835	2.1868	

Closed 8.1850 Reopened 11.1852

	Opened (Pass)	Closed (Pass)	Closed (Goods)
Dunston	1.1.1909	open	

Closed 1.5.1918 Reopened 1.10.1919
Closed 4.5.1926 Reopened 1.10.1984
Used for evacuation specials in World War II
Named Dunston-on-Tyne until 4.5.1926

	Opened (Pass)	Closed (Pass)	Closed (Goods)
MetroCentre	3.8.1987	open	

Gateshead MetroCentre renamed 17.5.1993

	Opened (Pass)	Closed (Pass)	Closed (Goods)
Blaydon	10.3.1835	open	

Temporary closure 3.9.1966 to 1.5.1967

	Opened (Pass)	Closed (Pass)	Closed (Goods)
Ryton	10.3.1835	5.7.1954	5.7.1954
Wylam	10.3.1835	open	26.4.1965

Temporary closure 3.9.1966 to 1.5.1967

	Opened (Pass)	Closed (Pass)	Closed (Goods)
Lemington	12.7.1875	15.9.1958	4.1.1960
Newburn	12.7.1875	15.9.1958	26.4.1965
Heddon-on-the-Wall	7.1881?	15.9.1958	15.9.1958
North Wylam	13.5.1876	11.3.1968	2.1.1961
Prudhoe	10.3.1835	open	26.4.1965
Mickley	11.1859	6.1915	

Previously untimetabled, serving Eltringham Colliery?

	Opened (Pass)	Closed (Pass)	Closed (Goods)
Stocksfield	10.3.1835	open	26.4.1965
Riding Mill	10.3.1835	open	26.4.1965
Corbridge	10.3.1835	open	26.4.1965
Hexham	10.3.1835	open	5.7.1991
Warden	28.6.1836	1.1837?	
Fourstones	1.1837?	2.1.1967	26.4.1965
Allerwash	28.6.1836	1.1837?	
Haydon Bridge (first)	28.6.1836	18.6.1838	
Haydon Bridge (second)	18.6.1838	open	26.4.1965
Bardon Mill	18.6.1838	open	26.4.1965
Haltwhistle	18.6.1838	open	
¶Blenkinsopp Hall Halt	18.6.1838	1875	
Greenhead	19.7.1836	2.1.1967	5.4.1965
Gilsland	19.7.1836	2.1.1967	5.4.1965

Rose Hill renamed 1.5.1869

	Opened (Pass)	Closed (Pass)	Closed (Goods)
Low Row	19.7.1836	5.1.1959	5.4.1965
Naworth	1.1871	5.5.1952	

Private station prior to 1871, probably from 7.1836

	Opened (Pass)	Closed (Pass)	Closed (Goods)
Brampton (Cumbria)	19.7.1836	open	5.7.1965

Milton renamed Brampton 1.9.1870, Brampton Jn 1.1.1885,
Brampton 30.4.1890, Brampton Jn 1.8.1913, Brampton
(Cumberland) 18.3.1971, Brampton (Cumbria) 5.4.1975

	Opened (Pass)	Closed (Pass)	Closed (Goods)
Brampton Town*	13.7.1836	29.10.1923	31.12.1923
Brampton Fell	19.7.1836?	by 1850	
How Mill	19.7.1836	5.1.1959	5.1.1959
Heads Nook	9.1862	2.1.1967	5.4.1965
Wetheral	19.7.1836	open	1.4.1955

Closed 2.1.1967 Reopened 5.10.1981

	Opened (Pass)	Closed (Pass)	Closed (Goods)
Scotby	19.7.1836	2.11.1959	2.11.1959

Hexham - Allendale

Opened
Hexham (Border Counties Jn) - Langley (Goods) 19.8.1867
Langley - Allendale (Goods) 1.1868
Hexham - Allendale (Passengers) 1.3.1869

Closed: Passengers 22.9.1930   **Closed: Goods** 20.11.1950

Stations	Opened (Pass)	Closed (Pass)	Closed (Goods)
Elrington Halt	1.3.1869	22.9.1930	20.11.1950

Elrington renamed 1.9.1926

Stations	Opened (Pass)	Closed (Pass)	Closed (Goods)
Langley	1.3.1869	22.9.1930	20.11.1950

Renamed Langley-on-Tyne from 29.7.1936

	Opened (Pass)	Closed (Pass)	Closed (Goods)
Staward	1.3.1869	22.9.1930	20.11.1950

Renamed Staward Halt from 1.4.1939

	Opened (Pass)	Closed (Pass)	Closed (Goods)
¶Bishopside Halt	*In working timetable 1938*		
Allendale	1.3.1869	22.9.1930	20.11.1950

Catton Road renamed 1.5.1898

Haltwhistle - Alston

Opened
Haltwhistle - Shaft Hill (Goods) 3.1851 (Passengers) 19.7.1851
Lambley - Alston (Goods) 5.1.1852 (Passengers) 21.5.1852
Haltwhistle - Lambley - Alston (All traffic) 17.11.1852

Closed: Goods 6.9.1965   **Closed: Passengers** 3.5.1976

Stations	Opened (Pass)	Closed (Pass)	Closed (Goods)
¶Plenmeller Halt*	by 1920	?	
¶Park Village	?	?	
Featherstone Park	19.7.1851	3.5.1976	23.8.1954

Featherstone renamed 1.1.1902   Halt 1933-37

	Opened (Pass)	Closed (Pass)	Closed (Goods)
Coanwood	19.7.1851	3.5.1976	19.9.1955

Shaft Hill closed 5.1853 Reopened as Shafthill 12.1862
Minor re-siting 1877/8   Renamed Coanwood 1.3.1885

	Opened (Pass)	Closed (Pass)	Closed (Goods)
Lambley	21.5.1852	3.5.1976	12.9.1960
¶Whitwham	?	?	
¶Softley	?	?	
¶Burnstones	?	?	
Slaggyford	21.5.1852	3.5.1976	19.9.1955
Alston	21.5.1852	3.5.1976	6.9.1965

Reopened by South Tynedale Railway (Narrow Gauge: 2ft 0in)
Alston 30.7.1983
Gilderdale Halt 12.1986 4.9.1999
Kirkhaugh Halt 4.9.1999

Hexham - Riccarton Junction
(Border Counties Railway: North British)

Opened
Hexham – Chollerford (Humshaugh) 5.4.1858
Chollerford - Countess Park 1.12.1859
Countess Park - Thorneyburn 1.2.1861
Thorneyburn - Falstone 2.9.1861
Falstone - Riccarton Jn (Goods) 24.6.1862 (Pass) 2.7.1862
Some sources: Falstone-Kielder op. 1.1.1862: others 12.5.1862

Closed: Passengers Hexham - Riccarton Jn 15.10.1956
Closed: Goods Hexham - Reedsmouth 1.9.1958
Bellingham - Riccarton Jn 1.9.1958
Reedsmouth – Bellingham 11.11.1963

Stations	Opened (Pass)	Closed (Pass)	Closed (Goods)
Wall	5.4.1858	19.9.1955	19.9.1955
Humshaugh	5.4.1858	15.10.1956	1.9.1958

Chollerford renamed 1.8.1919

	Opened (Pass)	Closed (Pass)	Closed (Goods)
Chollerton	1.12.1859	15.10.1956	1.9.1958
Barrasford	1.12.1859	15.10.1956	1.9.1958
Wark	1.12.1859	15.10.1956	1.9.1958
Countess Park	1.12.1859	1.2.1861	
Reedsmouth (first)	1.5.1861	1.11.1864	
Reedsmouth (second)	1.11.1864	15.10.1956	11.11.1963
Bellingham (North Tyne)	1.2.1861	15.10.1956	11.11.1963

Bellingham renamed 21.9.1926

Station	Opened	Closed	Closed
Charlton	1.2.1861	1.10.1862	
Tarset	1.2.1861	15.10.1956	1.9.1958
Thorneyburn	1.2.1861	15.10.1956	
Falstone	2.9.1861	15.10.1956	1.9.1958
Plashetts	By 1.7.1862	15.10.1956	1.9.1958
Lewiefield Halt	3.7.1933	15.10.1956	
Kielder Forest	By 1.7.1862	15.10.1956	1.9.1958

Kielder renamed 1.10.1948

Deadwater	1.3.1880	15.10.1956	19.9.1955

Opened privately as Deadwater Foot Crossing by 3.1877

Saughtree	1.7.1862	15.10.1956	1.9.1958

Closed (passengers) 1.12.1944 to 23.8.1948

Riccarton Junction	1.7.1862	6.1.1969	6.2.1967

Workmen's service began 2.6.1862
Riccarton renamed 1.1.1905

Morpeth - Reedsmouth
(Wansbeck Railway: North British)
Scotsgap - Rothbury
(Northumberland Central Railway: North British)

Opened		
Morpeth - Scotsgap	23.7.1862
Scotsgap – Knowesgate	10.1863
Knowesgate – Reedsmouth	1.5.1865
Scotsgap - Rothbury	1.11.1870

Closed: Passengers	Morpeth – Rothbury / Reedsmouth	
		15.9.1952
Closed: Goods	Scotsgap - Rothbury	11.11.1963
	Woodburn – Reedsmouth	11.11.1963
	Morpeth– Woodburn	3.10.1966

Stations	Opened (Pass)	Closed (Pass)	Closed (Goods)
Meldon	23.7.1862	15.9.1952	11.11.1963
Angerton	23.7.1862	15.9.1952	11.11.1963
Middleton North	23.7.1862	15.9.1952	11.11.1963

Middleton renamed 9.7.1923

Scotsgap, for Cambo	23.7.1862	15.9.1952	3.10.1966

Scot's Gap renamed 10.1903

Knowesgate	10.1863	15.9.1952	3.10.1966

Some sources state passenger opening was 1.7.1864
Knowe's Gate renamed 1.1908

¶Parsons Platform	?	In use 1937	

Also known as Ray House Halt

¶Summit Cottages	?	?	
Woodburn	1.5.1865	15.9.1952	3.10.1966
¶Vickers Platform	by 1910	15.9.1952	
Longwitton	1873	15.9.1952	11.11.1963

Private station from 1.11.1870 until 1873
Rothley renamed 4.1875

Ewesley	1.11.1870	15.9.1952	see Fontburn
Fontburn Halt	12.1.1903	15.9.1952	11.11.1963

Untimetabled private platform before 12.1.1903.
Whitehouse Platform renamed Fontburn 1.5.1904
Closed (Passengers) 3.10.1921
Reopened 21.11.1921 as Fontburn Halt.
Goods renamed Ewesley Siding 3.10.1921

Brinkburn Halt	1.11.1870	15.9.1952	11.11.1963

Brinkburn renamed 27.9.1948

Rothbury	1.11.1870	15.9.1952	11.11.1963

T. 1968 (HD)

THE FINAL TRAIN 1958

BRITISH RAILWAYS

IN CONJUNCTION WITH

The Ramblers' Association (Northern Area)

Conducted Rambles from Bellingham, Tarset, Kielder, Deadwater, Riccarton and Shankend †

(For routes see over)

RAMBLES available for individuals as well as organised parties
(Leaders provided)

Special Ramblers' Excursion by Diesel Train to
REEDSMOUTH, BELLINGHAM, TARSET, FALSTONE, KIELDER FOREST, DEADWATER, RICCARTON JUNCTION, SHANKEND † and HAWICK
SUNDAY 7th SEPTEMBER

OUTWARD		SECOND CLASS RETURN FARES.									RETURN	
		Reeds-mouth	Bellingham	Tarset	Falstone	Kielder Forest	Dead-water	Riccarton Jct.	Shankend†	Hawick		
NEWCASTLE ...dep.	a.m. 9 40	s.d. 6/3	s.d. 6/9	s.d. 7/0	s.d. 7/9	s.d. 8/9	s.d. 8/9	s.d. 9/6	s.d. 11/0	s.d. 11/6	Hawick ....dep.	p.m. 6 50
											Riccarton Jct. ..	7 20
											Deadwater	7 30
											Kielder Forest ..	7 40
											Falstone	8 0
											Tarset	8 10
											Bellingham	8 15
ARRIVAL TIMES		a.m. 11 10	a.m. 11 22	a.m. 11 30	a.m. 11 43	p.m. 12 5	p.m. 12 13	p.m. 12‡36	p.m. 12‡36	p.m. 12 46	Reedsmouth	8 30
											NEWCASTLE arr.	9 58

†THE TRAIN WILL STOP AT SHANKEND ON THE OUTWARD JOURNEY ONLY IN CONNECTION WITH THE CONDUCTED RAMBLE WHICH RETURNS FROM RICCARTON JUNCTION. IT WILL NOT STOP AT SHANKEND ON THE RETURN JOURNEY.

LIGHT REFRESHMENTS WILL BE AVAILABLE IN EACH DIRECTION
SERVED BY AN ATTENDANT PASSING DOWN THE TRAIN

ACCOMMODATION IS LIMITED AND PASSENGERS ARE REQUESTED TO BOOK IN ADVANCE

Children under three years of age, free ; three years & under 14 years, half-fares.

TICKETS CAN BE OBTAINED IN ADVANCE
FROM THE STATIONS AND ACCREDITED RAIL TICKET AGENCIES

Further information will be supplied on application to the stations, agencies, or to S. Cott District Passenger Superintendent, British Railways—Newcastle, Tel. 2-0741.

CONDITIONS OF ISSUE

These tickets are issued subject to the Regulations and Conditions in the Commission's Publications and Notices applicable to British Railways. Luggage allowances are as set out in the Conditions.

Published by British Railways (N.E. Region)—8/58   Printed in Great Britain   T.P.W. Ltd. N/cle—C5
PLEASE TURN OVER